THE EPIC OF UNITARIANISM

THE EPIC OF UNITARIANISM:

Original Writings from the History of Liberal Religion

David B. Parke

BOSTON: Skinner House Books

Library of Congress catalog card number 57-7797
Printed in the United States of America

Published by Skinner House Books. Skinner House Books is an imprint of
the Unitarian Universalist Association, a liberal religious organization with
more than 1,000 congregations in the U.S. and Canada. 25 Beacon Street,
Boston, MA 02108-2800.

ISBN 1-55896-246-8

13 12
06 05 04

Note: The Unitarian Universalist Association is committed to using gender-inclusive language in all of its publications. In this edition, all introductory matter and connecting commentary have been revised to conform to gender-inclusive language. In the interest of historical authenticity the documents quoted are printed, as in the first edition of this work, in their original form.

To the memory of
EARL MORSE WILBUR
Faithful scholar
Gracious friend

He has flung wide
the gates of history
that we may pass through.

It is a curious error to suppose you
can carry on effectively a great
liberal tradition while remaining
at the same time ignorant, or almost
ignorant, of the beliefs and
achievements of the people who have
handed that tradition over to you.

Harry C. Meserve

Contents

The Twentieth Century: Humanism and Theism in a New Age

Note: Page numbers in this Contents section refer the reader to
the beginning of each excerpted document. All documents are
preceded by contemporary commentary, which appears in itali-
cized text.

A New Foreword

This work, first published in May 1957, has been continuously in print since that date. It was degenderized in 1985 but otherwise, except for one or two corrections involving dates, has not been revised.

I conceived of this project in the fall of 1952 as a graduate student at the University of Chicago. The second volume of Earl Morse Wilbur's *History of Unitarianism* having appeared that year, I wanted to get behind Wilbur's narrative prose to the original writings of those who had made the history. Aware of the formative power of the Hebrew prophets in the development of Israel, and of the gospels in the development of Christianity, I decided to search out and publish the formative documents of Unitarian and Universalist history, as an extended footnote, as it were, to Wilbur's work. Beacon Press, then directed by Melvin Arnold, was receptive. I started reading, consulted my professors and colleagues, and led workshops on Unitarian history at summer youth conferences. Newly settled in November 1955 at the Unitarian Church of Peterborough, NH (which granted me a timely leave of absence for the purpose), I completed the manuscript in the fall of 1956.

What would I change if I were doing it again?

A classic has been defined as something that doesn't have to be rewritten. In place of the severely edited versions included here, I would include the full text of Channing's Baltimore Sermon (1819), Emerson's Divinity School Address (1838), and Parker's South Boston Sermon (1841). It is perhaps no coincidence that Beacon Press published *Three Prophets of Religious Liberalism: Channing, Emerson, Parker* in 1961, a year after this work appeared in a paperback edition.

I would incorporate more women's voices—including Judith Sargent Murray's writings on women's rights, Margaret Fuller's journals and letters, Elizabeth Palmer Peabody's views on childhood, and the writings of Mary Augusta Safford, Caroline Bartlett Crane, and other members of the Iowa Sisterhood. I would include Anna Garlin Spencer's views on the role of women in marriage, family, and marketplace, and Sophia Lyon Fahs's writings on religious education. Thirty years ago a colleague reproached me for omitting Fahs's "A New Ministry to Children" (1945). He was right to do so.

I would rethink the place of Michael Servetus (or Miguel Serveto) in the emergence of Unitarianism and Socinianism in the sixteenth century. I now believe that Servetus' life, death, and writings on the Trinity constituted the occasion rather than the cause of the anti-Trinitarian and tolerationist impulses which led to the establishment of the Unitarian movement in Transylvania and of the Minor Reformed Church in Poland. In this connection, I would revise my treatment of John Calvin and Calvinism. The antecedents of New England Unitarianism, including English and American Puritanism and Separatism and Dutch Arminianism, were expressions of moderate Calvinism. In the spirit of the Genevan reforms these movements emphasized the sovereignty of God, the sufficiency of the scriptures, and the rule of the saints. To the extent that the modern principles of individualism, plenary grace, self-government, and the right of revolution derive from Reformed principles in theology and church government, Calvin is a precursor of Unitarianism. It is bad history, I now realize, to portray Calvin chiefly as the antagonist of Servetus.

What events subsequent to 1957 would I include in a new edition? The 1961 merger of the Unitarian and Universalist bodies into the Unitarian Universalist Association is one. The emergence of the Black Unitarian Universalist Caucus in 1967 and the vote of the 1968 and 1969 UUA General Assemblies to fund a biracial Black Affairs Council is another. On a larger canvas, I would measure the impact of the Holocaust on ethics, the impact of experimental science and existentialism on theology, and the impact of Protestant and Catholic ecumenism on the doctrine of the church. The impact of the Cold War, the Third World, and the women's revolution on the dynamics of power, and the impact of quantum theory, psychoanalysis, and brain research on the concept of mind—these also cry out for recognition in the community of faith.

I conclude with a question to readers. Why is it that no major theological controversy has engaged Unitarian Universalists since the humanist-theist controversy early in this century?

David B. Parke
Salem, Massachusetts
January 16, 1992

The Sixteenth Century: Antitrinitarianism and Toleration

Until the sixteenth century western Europe was Roman Catholic. A few scattered groups—the Waldenses, Hussites, and Bogomils, to name three—had rebelled against the Church, but without widespread effect. The first cataclysmic protest against Catholicism was initiated in 1517 by a German monk, Martin Luther, who held that persons were justified not by submission to the Church but by faith in God. When his protests resulted in excommunication, Luther assumed the leadership of a new religious movement, Protestantism.

The Protestant Reformation spread quickly to Switzerland, Italy, France, the Low Countries, and Scandinavia. Seeing in it an ally against oppression of every kind, princes, peasants, merchants, and scholars flocked to the new movement which, however, grew so rapidly that it was impossible for one person to control it. The Lutheran Reformation was more than an ecclesiastical revolution. By sundering Catholicism's structure of authority it precipitated a social upheaval out of which, in the succeeding centuries, European Nationalism, modern democracy, and capitalistic civilization have emerged.

Every revolution that seeks to effect permanent changes in the social structure must retain elements of continuity from the old social structure. For the early reformers, especially Luther and John Calvin, uniformity of Christian doctrine was such an element. After wavering, they chose to retain the Catholic doctrines virtually intact —excluding those ascribing supreme authority to the Roman pope. One of the items retained was the Athanasian creed.* But many Protestants, especially Anabaptists in Germany, Switzerland, and Holland, were dissatisfied with the traditional dogmas. Believing that the Bible should be the only rule of faith, they held that Christian doctrine needed a reformation too. The first strong voice of radical

---

* A fifth-century formulation of what it meant to be a Christian. The Athanasian Creed reads in part:

"3. Now the catholic faith is this: that we worship one God in a Trinity, and the Trinity is a unity;

"4. Neither confounding the persons, nor dividing the substance.

"5. For there is one person of the Father, another of the Son, another of the Holy Spirit.

"6. But the divinity of the Father, and of the Son, and of the Holy Spirit, is one, the glory equal, the majesty co-eternal."

1

Protestantism was that of a Spaniard, Michael Servetus. The epic of Unitarianism begins with him.

When, in 1517, Martin Luther hammered his ninety-five theses on the door of Wittenberg Cathedral, Michael Servetus (1511-1553) was a six-year-old Catholic boy living in Villanueva, in northern Spain. He was the son of the local judge and showed exceptional ability at an early age. Although his father wanted him to be a lawyer, two experiences changed Michael Servetus' life.

While studying law in France, Servetus read a Bible for the first time. In it he found only scanty basis for the traditional dogmas of the Church, and no sound basis at all for the doctrine of the Trinity. He discovered also that the Jesus of the Gospels differed markedly from the Jesus of the Christian creeds.

A year later in Bologna Servetus watched the Pope crown Spain's Charles V as Roman emperor. Of the experience he later wrote, "With these very eyes I saw him [the Pope] borne with pomp on the shoulders of princes, and in the public streets adored by the whole people kneeling, to such a point that those that succeeded even in kissing his feet or his shoes deemed themselves happy beyond the rest. Oh, beast of beasts the most wicked! Most shameless of harlots!"

Servetus' reaction against the incomprehensible theology and worldly corruption of the Church focussed on the doctrine of the Trinity. As a brash youth of twenty, he set out to convince the leaders of the Protestant movement that they were wrong about the Trinity, and that he was right. When his letters and conversations failed to move them, he presented his case in a learned, shrewd, and impertinent book, On the Errors of the Trinity (1531).[1]

In investigating the holy mysteries of the divine Triad, I have thought that one ought to start from the man; for I see most men approaching their lofty speculation about the Word without having any fundamental understanding of CHRIST, and they attach little or no importance to the man, and give the true CHRIST quite over to oblivion. But I shall endeavor to recall to their memories who the

CHRIST is. However, what and how much importance is to be attached to CHRIST, the Church shall decide.

Seeing that the pronoun indicates a man, whom they call the human nature, I shall admit these three things: first, this man is JESUS CHRIST; second, he is the Son of God; third, he is God. . . .

. . . CHRIST himself bears witness that the works that he does sufficiently show that he has been sent by the Father. And Nathanael, from his saying, "I saw thee underneath the fig tree," concludes that he is the Son of God who was to be sent as King of Israel. They draw a similar conclusion from his stilling the wind; and from the miracles that he did, Peter concludes, "We know that thou art CHRIST, the Son of the living God."

These conclusions also clearly prove what I said in the second place: namely, that he whom I call CHRIST is the Son of God; for from the miracles that he did they conclude that he is the Son of God. And it having been proved that he is JESUS CHRIST, this turns out as proved; for one who denies that he is the Son denies JESUS CHRIST, since Scripture proclaims nothing else than that JESUS CHRIST is the Son of God. Moreover, by many testimonies of the Scriptures he is shown to be especially the Son, and God is called Father with regard to him—really a Father, I say—because he was begotten by one filling the place of a human father. For he was not begotten of the seed of Joseph, as Carpocrates, Cerinthus, and Photinus wickedly and falsely declared. But instead of the seed of a man, the almighty power of the Word of God overshadowed Mary, the Holy Spirit acting within her; and it continues, "Wherefore also that which is born shall be called holy, the Son of God. . . ."

In the third place, I said that this proposition is true: CHRIST is God, for he is said to be God in appearance, because, as the Apostle says, "he was in the form of God." And, according to Tertullian, he was found to be God through his power, just as he was man through his flesh. For CHRIST after the inward man (to speak in the manner of Paul) means something divine, resulting from an inward anointing divinely done. According to the flesh, he is man; and in the spirit he is God, because "that which is born of the Spirit is spirit," and, "God is a Spirit." And, "Unto us a child is born . . . his name shall be called . . . Mighty God." See clearly that both the name and the might of God are attributed to a child that is born, unto whom "hath been given all authority in heaven and on earth." And Thomas calls him, "My God, my Lord." And CHRIST is called, God in all things to be praised and blessed. And in many other passages is his divinity shown, because he was exalted that he might receive divinity, and the name above every name. . . .

The philosophers have invented besides a third separate being, truly and really distinct from the other two, which they call the third Person, or the Holy Spirit; and thus they have contrived an imaginary Trinity, three beings in one Nature. But in reality three beings, three Gods, or one threefold God, are foisted upon us under the pretense and with the names of a unity. On this matter hear the view of recent writers which John Major states in his *Sentences*. For with them it is very easy, taking the words in their strict sense, for three beings to exist which they say are strictly, simply, truly and really so different or distinct that one is born of another, and one is breathed out by the others, and all these three are shut up in one jar. I, however, since I am unwilling to misuse the word Persons, shall call them the first *being*, the second being, the third being; for in the Scriptures I find no other name for them, and what is properly to be thought of the Persons I shall say later on. Admitting, therefore, these three, which after their own fashion they call Persons, by reasoning from the lower to the higher they freely admit a plurality of beings, a plurality of entities, a plurality of Essences, a plurality of *Ousias* [i.e., substances], and in consequence, taking the word, God, strictly, they will have a plurality of Gods.

If this is so, why are the Tritoites blamed, who say that there are three Gods? For they also contrive three Gods, or one threefold one. These three Gods of theirs form one composite Ousia; and although some will not use a word implying that the three have been put together, yet they do use a word implying that they are constituted together, and that God is constituted out of the three beings. It is clear, therefore, that we are Tritoites, and we have a threefold God: we have become Atheists, that is, men without any God. For as soon as we try to think about God, we are turned aside to three phantoms, so that no kind of unity remains in our conception. But what else is being without God but being unable to think about God, when there is always presented to our understanding a haunting kind of confusion of three beings, by which we are forever deluded into supposing that we are thinking about God . . . They seem to be living in another world while they dream of such things; for the kingdom of heaven knows none of this nonsense, and it is in another way, unknown to them, that Scripture speaks of the Holy Spirit. . . .

. . . There are three wonderful *dispositions* of God, in each of which his divinity shines forth; and from this you might very well understand a Trinity. For the Father is the whole substance and the one God from whom these degrees and personations proceed. And they are three, not by virtue of some distinction of beings in God, but through an *oikonomia* [disposition] of God in various forms of Deity; for the same divinity which is in the Father is communicated to the Son, JESUS CHRIST, and to our spirits, which are the temples of the living God; for the Son and our sanctified spirits are sharers with us in the Substance of the Father, are its members, pledges, and instruments; although the kind of deity in them is varying, and this is why they are called distinct Persons, that is, manifold aspects, diverse forms and kinds, of deity. . . .

. . . How much this tradition of the Trinity has, alas! been a laughing-stock to the Mohammedans, only God knows. The Jews also shrink from giving adherence to this fancy of ours, and laugh at our foolishness about the Trinity; and on account of its blasphemies they do not believe that this is the Messiah who was promised in their law. And not only Mohammedans and Hebrews, but the very beasts of the field, would make fun of us did they grasp our fantastical notion, for all the works of the Lord bless the one God. . . .

This most burning plague, therefore, was added and superimposed, as were the new gods which have recently come, which our fathers did not worship. And this plague of philosophy was brought upon us by the Greeks, for they above all other men are most given to philosophy; and we, hanging upon their lips, have also become philosophers. Perhaps some will deem it a slight fault if I admit that they may have erred. But I prove this in no other way than by showing that they never understood the passages of the Scriptures which they adduce with regard to this matter. If they distinguished the brightness that then was from their own darkness so utterly confused, they might realize that Paul well said that the Church of God is the ground and pillar of the truth; which is no more than to say that the word of the Gospel is true; and the word of the Gospel is this, namely, that JESUS CHRIST is the son of God.

[Of the Holy Spirit I say] that our spirit dwelling in us is God his very self; and that this is the Holy Spirit in us, according to the saying of the prophet, is shown by the Apostle, saying, "The Spirit of God in us," because God said, "I will dwell in them." And he who contemns us contemns God, because he put his Spirit in us; and he who lies to the Holy Spirit lies not to men but to God. And herein we bear witness a certain heavenly feeling, and a hidden divine something, for when it bloweth where it will, I hear the voice thereof, but know not whence it cometh, or whither it goeth; and so is every one that is born of the Spirit.

With regard to the Holy Spirit, I speak of an appearance in bodily form, in consequence of the Spirit's descending; but I speak of a disposition in us, and the former is limited to the latter. Hence I always say that the Holy Spirit is the activity of God in the spirit of man; and that outside of man it is not properly called the Holy Spirit. . . .

. . . And so I admit one Person of the Father, another Person of the Son, another Person of the Holy Spirit; and I admit Father, Son, and Holy Spirit, three Persons in one Godhead; and this is the true Trinity. But I should prefer not to use a word foreign to the Scriptures, lest perchance in future the philosophers have occasion to go astray. And I have no controversy with the earlier writers, because they employed this word sensibly. But may this blasphemous and philosophical distinction of three beings in one God be rooted out from the minds of men. . . .

Servetus' book was a best-seller. It ignited smoldering embers of Antitrinitarian sentiment in Germany, Switzerland, and especially in Italy, where a number of Protestant dissenters had gathered, later to produce some of the leaders of Polish Antitrinitarianism.

But the Reformers, whom Servetus had hoped to convert, recoiled in shock and dismay. They were shocked by his effrontery and insults, dismayed at what his views might do to the young Protestant movement if left unchecked. The Reformers also feared a renewal of Catholic suppressions if Protestant doctrine deviated too far. Thus Servetus, while intending the opposite, forced the Protestant leaders to embrace the Trinity ever more zealously.

Almost immediately the sale of Servetus' book was forbidden in leading Protestant cities. The Spanish Inquisition sought unsuccess-

fully to bring him to trial. Servetus, alarmed and disappointed by the unfavorable reaction to his work, published in 1532 a "corrected" version of his views, but the corrections were minor and he remained a religious outcast.

Between 1532 and 1553 Servetus lived in France under an assumed name—Michael Villanovanus. He succeeded brilliantly as an editor and doctor and gave lectures at the University of Paris. But, fatally attracted to theology, he reopened a correspondence with Calvin, hoping to show him his errors. Calvin resented Servetus' criticisms and came to hate him. Servetus at this time was writing his master work, The Restoration of Christianity, which offered a plan for the complete reformation of the Christian churches—Catholic and Protestant alike—based on the teachings of Jesus.

With the publication of The Restoration of Christianity, "Michael Villanovanus" was exposed as the heretic Servetus. The French Inquisition imprisoned him, but he escaped. En route to Naples, Italy, where he had friends, he passed through Geneva, but was recognized and immediately arrested. Calvin, who had once boasted that should Servetus ever come to Geneva he would never let him get away alive, had his man.

Servetus, rotting in prison, was tried before the Council of Judges (Syndics) in Geneva. Calvin kept in the background, participating in the case only enough to be sure Servetus would be found guilty. Sentence was pronounced on October 26, 1553.[2] Servetus died in flames the following noon.

The sentence pronounced against Michel Servet de Villeneufve of the Kingdom of Aragon in Spain who some twenty-three or twenty-four years ago printed a book at Hagenau in Germany against the Holy Trinity containing many great blasphemies to the scandal of the said churches of Germany, the which book he freely confesses to have printed in the teeth of the remonstrances made to him by the learned and evangelical doctors of Germany. In consequence he became a fugitive from Germany. Nevertheless he continued in his errors and, in order the more to spread the venom of his heresy, he printed secretly a book in Vienne of Dauphiny full of the said heresies and horrible, execrable blasphemies against the Holy Trinity, against the Son of God, against the baptism of infants and the foundations of the Christian religion. He confesses that in this book he called believers in the Trinity Trinitarians and atheists. He calls this Trinity a diabolical monster with three heads. He blasphemes detestably against the Son of God, saying that Jesus Christ is not the Son of God from eternity. He calls infant baptism an invention of the devil and sorcery. His execrable blasphemies are scandalous against the majesty of God, the Son of God and the Holy Spirit. This entails the murder and ruin of many souls. Moreover he wrote a letter to one of our ministers in which, along with other numerous blasphemies, he declared our holy evangelical religion to be without faith and without God and that in place of God we have a three-headed Cerberus. He confesses that because of this abominable book he was made a prisoner at Vienne and perfidiously escaped. He has been burned there in effigy together with five bales of his books. Never-the-less, having been in prison in our city, he persists maliciously in his detestable errors and calumniates true Christians and faithful followers of the immaculate Christian tradition.

Wherefore we Syndics, judges of criminal cases in this city, having witnessed the trial conducted before us at the instance of our Lieutenant against you "Michel Servet de Villeneufve" of the Kingdom of Aragon in Spain, and having seen your voluntary and repeated confessions and your books, judge that you, Servetus, have for a long time promulgated false and thoroughly heretical doctrine, despising all remonstrances and corrections and that you have with malicious and perverse obstinacy sown and divulged even in printed books opinions against God the Father, the Son and the Holy Spirit, in a word against the fundamentals of the Christian religion, and that you have tried to make a schism and trouble the Church of God by which many souls may have been ruined and lost, a thing horrible, shocking, scandalous and infectious. And you have had neither shame nor horror of setting yourself against the divine Majesty and the Holy Trinity, and so you have obstinately tried to infect the world with your stinking heretical poison. . . . For these and other reasons, desiring to purge the Church of God of such infection and cut off the rotten member, having taken counsel with our citizens and having invoked the name of God to give just judgment . . . having God and the Holy Scriptures before our eyes, speaking in the name of the Father, Son and Holy Spirit, we now in writing give final sentence and condemn you, Michael Servetus, to be bound and taken to Champel and there attached to a stake and burned with your book to ashes. And so you shall finish your days and give an example to others who would commit the like.

"Scarcely were his ashes cold before there arose a controversy over the punishment of heretics." So wrote the reformer Beza. The image of Servetus dying in flames, just because his view of the Trinity differed from Calvin's, caused a storm of outrage. Calvin cried that "the dogs are barking at me on all sides," and was almost forced to leave Geneva. To justify himself he hastily wrote a Defense of the Orthodox Faith respecting the Holy Trinity, against the prodigious errors of . . . Servetus early in 1554. Believing heresy to be worse than murder, Calvin argued that Servetus had to be put to death, else his heresy contaminate all Christendom. But there were other voices, of which Sebastian Castellio's was the loudest.

Castellio (1515-1563) was a learned and fearless Frenchman who had worked alongside Calvin in Geneva until, because of his liberal views, he was forced to leave the city. Now a professor at Basel, the center of Swiss liberalism, he decided to speak out against persecution and to reassert the right of conscience in religion. Castellio found that the church fathers and the Reformers—including Luther —were almost unanimous in condemning the death penalty for heretics. So he collected their opinions into a book entitled Concerning Heretics, whether they are to be persecuted and how they are to be treated (1554).[3]

Here are portions of Castellio's dedication to the Duke Christolph of Württemberg, and an excerpt from Luther.

When I consider the life and teaching of Christ who, though innocent Himself, yet always pardoned the guilty and told us to pardon until seventy times seven, I do not see how we can retain the name of Christian if we do not imitate His clemency and mercy. Even if we were innocent we ought to follow Him. How much more when we are covered with so many sins? When I examine my own life I see so many and such great sins that I do not think I could even obtain pardon from my Savior if I were thus ready to condemn others. Let each one examine himself, sound and search his conscience, and weigh his thoughts, words, and deeds. Then will he see himself as one who is not in a position to remove the mote from the eye of his brother before he has taken the beam from his own. In view of the many sins which are laid to us all, the best course, would be for each to look to himself, to exercise care for the correction of his life and not for the condemnation of others. This license of judgment which reigns everywhere today, and fills all with blood, constrains me, most Clement Prince, to do my best to staunch the blood, especially that blood which is so wrongfully shed,—I mean the blood of those who are called heretics, which name has become today so infamous, detestable, and horrible that there is no quicker way to dispose of an enemy than to accuse him of heresy. The mere word stimulates such horror that when it is pronounced men shut their ears to the victim's defense, and furiously persecute not merely the man himself, but also those who dare to open their mouths on his behalf; by which rage it has come to pass that many have been destroyed before their cause was really understood.

Now I say this not because I favor heretics. I hate heretics. But I speak because I see here two great dangers. And the first is that he be held for a heretic, who is not a heretic. This happened in former times, for Christ and his disciples were put to death as heretics, and there is grave reason to fear a recurrence in our century, which is not better, but rather worse. The danger is greater because Christ said, "Think not that I am come to send peace on earth; I came not to send peace, but a sword. For I am come to set a man at variance against his father, and the daughter against her mother," etc. You see how easy it is for calumniators to say of a Christian, "This man is seditious. He sets a son at variance against his father and disturbs the public peace." Great care must be exercised to distinguish those who are really seditious from Christians. Outwardly they do the same thing and are judged guilty of the same crime by those who do not understand. Christ was crucified among thieves.

The other danger is that he who is really a heretic be punished more severely or in a manner other than that required by Christian discipline. For these reasons I have collected in this book the opinions of many who have written on this matter, in order that a consideration of their arguments may lead to less offense for the future. . . .

[Addressed to Christ:] O Creator and King of the world, dost Thou see these things? Art Thou become so changed, so cruel, so contrary to Thyself? When Thou was on earth none was more mild, more clement, more patient of injury. As a sheep before the shearer Thou wast dumb. When scourged, spat upon, mocked, crowned with thorns, and crucified shamefully among thieves, Thou didst pray for them who did Thee this wrong. Art Thou now so changed? I beg Thee in the name of Thy Father, dost Thou now command that those who do not understand Thy precepts as the mighty demand, be drowned in water, cut with lashes to the entrails, sprinkled with salt, dismembered by the sword, burned at a slow fire, and otherwise tortured in every manner and as long as possible? Dost Thou, O Christ, command and approve of these things? Are they Thy vicars who make these sacrifices? Art Thou present when they summon Thee and dost Thou eat human flesh? If Thou, Christ, dost these things or if Thou commandest that they be done, what hast Thou left for the devil? Dost Thou the very same things as Satan? O blasphemies and shameful audacity of men, who dare to attribute to Christ that which they do by the command and at the instigation of Satan! But I will restrain myself. I think, Prince, you already sufficiently understand how far such deeds are contrary to the teaching and practice of Christ. Let us then, now hear the opinions of others. You will find them speaking, however, as if it were already clear who are the true heretics.

[Castellio quotes from Martin Luther's treatise "On Civil Government":] Heresy is a spiritual thing which can be cut with no iron, burned with no fire, drowned with no water. Only with the Word of God can it be cut, burned and drowned, as Paul says in II Corinthians 10, "The weapons of our warfare are not carnal, but mighty through God to the pulling down of strongholds, casting down the imaginations and every high thing that exalteth itself against the knowledge of God, bringing into captivity every thought to the Obedience of Christ."

Moreover, faith and heresy are never so entrenched as when they are opposed by sheer violence apart from the Word of God, for everyone can see that such violence lacks a just cause, since it proceeds without the Word of God, and can defend itself only by pure force like a brute beast. Even in civil affairs force has no place unless injustice has already been convicted by justice. How much more is it impossible to proceed in these exalted and arduous cases by sheer violence without justice and the word of God? See what wise lords these are who wish to drive out heresy, but succeed only in fortifying their enemies and making themselves suspect and in the wrong. Would you eliminate heresy, then you must devise a plan to pluck it from the heart and root it out of the desires. With force you will merely entrench, not expel. What have you accomplished if you confirm heresy in the heart and weaken it only on the tongue and drive men to lies? But if you strive with the Word of God, this will enlighten the heart and all heresy and error will vanish of itself.

Beside Servetus, there were other heretics who opposed the Catholic and Protestant orthodoxies of their time. Gribaldi in Switzerland and Germany, Gentile in Switzerland and Poland, and Schwenckfeld in Germany were three of the most important. Brilliant, devout, and courageous, they were also condemned and imprisoned—"prophets without honor in their own countries." Because of their non-conforming personalities and perilous circumstances they worked alone, each pursuing a singular reformation.

Caspar Schwenckfeld (1489-1561) was in many respects a German Servetus. As a youth he had studied law only to become fascinated with theological questions. Like Servetus he met and corresponded with the Reformers but became critical of them and set out on his own. He was a voluntary exile from his native Silesia as Servetus had been from Spain. Both were laypersons; both devoted themselves to what they regarded as the service of Christ regardless of personal consequences.

Theologically many of their views coincided, especially on the nature of Christ (both held him to be a man, the Son of God) and the Holy Spirit (both believed it to be God's presence in humankind). It is possible that they influenced each other, for they met several times. They differed as to the channel of God's truth, Servetus stressing Scripture as the vehicle, whereas Schwenckfeld believed that God speaks his truth through the Holy Spirit to our hearts directly. Faith is not so much believing as participating in God. In this Schwenckfeld anticipated the Transcendentalism of Emerson, Parker, and the Concord school three centuries later. For Schwenckfeld, prayer and meditation were surer paths to the Christian life than preaching and the sacraments; he refrained from taking communion because of its lack of seriousness and sincerity.

Temperamentally Servetus and Schwenckfeld were, however, opposites, the former quarrelsome and unpredictable, the latter tolerant and persuasive.

In further contrast to Servetus, who attracted no personal disciples to carry on his ideas, the Schwenckfelder church has maintained a continuous existence for almost four hundred years in Germany and later in the United States, voicing in worship, education, and book-publishing Schwenckfeld's ideal of spiritual and undogmatic Christianity.

Schwenckfeld believed that the church was the realm of the inward spirit ruled by Christ, the state the realm of outward forms ruled by women and men. Both were necessary, but they should not interfere with each other. The following selection on "The Office and Scope of Civil Government" is from a letter written by Schwenckfeld in 1548 to the chief judge in Strasbourg, France. A clear statement of the suitable relations of church and state, it appears here for the first time in English.[4]

May the grace of our Lord Jesus Christ, the true Son of God, be multiplied in your heart. I proffer my Christian and willing service first of all, most wise, honorable sir and friend.

I received your letter with sincere pleasure, and praise the Lord that He has endowed your prudence with such Christian zeal in these dangerous times; that you finally are concerned about your soul's salvation; and that in your office you would like to act according to the will of God. Wherefore I was occasioned, in answer to your high and Christian request, to indicate to you my humble opinion and consideration about the office of secular power, but with this condition, that neither you nor anyone else accuse me that in the following opinion I would drive out of Christianity and reject civil authority because I maintain and write that so far as the office is concerned, it does not belong into the kingdom of grace of Christ our Lord, to carry on there with force, laws, and prohibitions, which is not my meaning in so far as civil authorities believe in Christ and live a Christian life, that they should, or might, not be Christians. But I indicate how the spiritual government, administration, and rule of the spiritual office of grace and of the kingdom of Christ belong solely to Christ Jesus the Son of God our Lord, which He conducts for the salvation of depraved man, in the Holy Spirit, for

He alone is the head of His Church and the King of His people. And in order that we may also thoroughly recognize what the office of civil authority is, how far it extends, and what it is as different from Christ's kingdom of grace and from His spiritual government over the soul and conscience as heaven is from earth. Although in time past you were otherwise instructed by certain preachers and learned persons, from which it resulted that the government at this time grievously wronged the regnant King, Christ, and His kingdom and people; they afterwards transgressed also against their highest government, all under the pretense of the word of God and the holy gospel. But civil government also is instituted and appointed by God, and the Lord Jesus Christ is a Lord of all governments and a King of all kings, since all power in heaven and on earth is given Him by the Father. Although your worldly office is appointed over life and property and does not belong into the spiritual kingdom of Christ, nor does it extend over the conscience, to rule the same, yet each one, personally (if he would be a Christian and be saved), is obliged to love the King of the kingdom of God, Jesus Christ, from whom their power comes, and to confess, and so far as they are able as Christians, to promote His divine truth. But they must not apply restraint and duress in Christendom, nor grieve anyone (who otherwise is peaceable) in matters of faith, nor drive out or kill, in order that they may not infringe on the office of the Lord Christ and fall into judgment and punishment, as happens today. May our Lord Jesus Christ the Lord of glory, make amends for every wrong, bring order out of chaos, and graciously protect and keep in His truth all who truly love Him, confess and worship His glory, and be gracious to all others and help them to a knowledge of the truth. Amen. My consideration follows.

In our time the State has been ill-informed and badly advised and has gone too far in that it permitted itself to maintain the religion of the Lord Christ and matters of Christian faith by the sword and by force. For, as far as its office is concerned, it has no right to rule the Christian religion, the word of God, and the holy gospel of Christ. That office belongs to another Lord and Ruler, namely, to the Son of God, Jesus Christ, our Lord and God, whom the heavenly Father has set as King and Head of His Church, Ps. 2; Eph. 1; Acts 20.

The office of temporal, carnal government or civil authority was not instituted by God the Lord that it should govern, rule and administer religion and the divine service of the New Testament, or that those persons who administer such office must be spiritual or Christian, but the office mentioned belongs into the order of the things of this world. Therefore, Peter calls it an ordinance of man that worldly peace, human justice, love and civil unanimity and supervision be thereby maintained, that men may live together, that the good be protected and the evil punished, 1 Pet. 2; Ro. 13.

God the Almighty Lord, provided the human race, honorable and good people, and particularly His children and Christians (although at this time, alas, there are few, and they are a refuse, an abomination, and a horror as were the children of Israel among the Egyptians), with the office of civil authority that they might have temporal peace, be safe from wicked, restless men and have rest and a place in the world as long as it pleased God; that they might praise God, serve Christ their Lord, and complete their pilgrimage according to the will of God.

The office of civil authority is a worldly office, of the order of these earthly things, has a special power, special judgment and law, belongs to a particular people, and is to be distinguished from the heavenly kingdom of Christ, from His spiritual rule, power, right, and order, yea, from the spiritual people of the New Testament, as widely as heaven and earth, although the people of the New Testament, that is, the true Christians, as far as their body and temporal possessions and life are concerned, are all included thereunder and are therefore obligated to be obedient and subject to the government as much as concerns its office.

Paul the holy apostle of Jesus Christ writes nothing in all his epistles about Christian government. This term has only recently been invented and devised for our benefit. He does not teach as some have done, that Papists shall be removed from the office of established government and Protestants be installed; that the kingdom of Christ our Lord be well conducted. He teaches, as stated in Romans Chapter 13, nothing other than that the Christians who are scattered hither and yon in the city of Rome shall be obedient to the government in those things which pertain to external office, as is emphatically stated there. Furthermore, that epistle was written in the time of the Emperor Nero. They shall be obedient, but not against God the Lord, nor against His Holy Word, Christ, and faith, to which the pasage in Acts pertains, where Peter says: We must obey God rather than man.

Our Lord Christ does not command anything more in the Gospel than that the Christians shall give to Caesar what is his, namely, the penny and due obedience, and as Paul says: Tribute, custom, fear and honor. But above all, they shall give to God what is God's, namely, the highest love, adoration, and right worship, trust, and true obedience to His Word, and to live in His fear. God the Lord wants the heart and demands true knowledge and recognition of His Holy Name, which is Jesus Christ our Lord. He demands of all Christians the fruits of good works and the testimony of a good conscience, and that they walk irreproachably before God and the world. . . .

The State is ill-informed and badly advised and misled in that as a worldly government with its worldly office and judgment, it wanted to rule and administer the kingdom of Christ which is not of this world. The Lord Christ speaks in opposition to this, saying: My kingdom is not of this world; if my kingdom were of this world then would my servants fight that I should not be delivered to the Jews, Jo. 18:36.

It is ill-informed and badly advised that as a worldly authority it has the official power to rule over the Christian faith with its appurtenances, which, however, is a gracious gift of God, as we have heard that not all have faith. It is not in its jurisdiction nor power either to command or forbid faith, as it also cannot give it to anyone nor take it away. It is also not in its jurisdiction to exterminate or expel the opponents of doctrine so long as they do not resort to the fist, or otherwise live peaceably; neither to uproot the tares and weeds and to judge with the sword, which is the office of Christ and His Holy Spirit and is also the service of the apostleship. He administers His office not with a physical sword but with the spiritual sword and Word of God, Mat. 13:24-30.

The State is ill-informed and badly advised in that as a worldly authority it has attached the spiritual to the worldly sword, and wanted to rule and administer the kingdom of Christ with the worldly sword, for which previous to this time, the Pope was censured most severely. But as the Pope administered the worldly kingdom and authority along with the spiritual, so the State has tried to rule the spiritual kingdom of Christ along with the worldly, erroneously and to the great corruption of many people, souls, and consciences.

It is ill-informed and badly advised in that it has permitted itself to be persuaded that the spiritual kingdom of our Lord Jesus Christ and the worldly, political kingdom, both of which move upon the earth yet each in its order, are one, although they are as widely different as heaven and earth, as flesh and spirit, as death and life, as temporal and eternal. God and our Lord Jesus Christ administer the worldly, temporal kingdom through the children of men, as He gave the earth to the children of men and reserved heaven for Himself. God administers and rules this visible world through emperor, king, prince, and lord, mayor, sovereign, and potentate, as through the heads or through their representative chiefs, officials, magistrate, and human regime; into their hands He gave the physical sword and committed the office of government, to preserve peace and unity on this earth; to rule land and people; to bring in tax, arms, and tribute; to create ways and means; to preserve land and cities, yea, to protect widows and orphans; to protect the good; to restrain the wicked; to distribute inheritance amongst brothers; and other things that pertain to the maintenance of this worldly regime, life and property, of which civil authority has its honor, obedience and reward, yea, obedience is owed to it for this reason, and not only because of chastisement but also for conscience's sake, Ro. 13:5.

But the eternal, spiritual and heavenly kingdom of Christ which has its beginning, continuation, and growth in faith among God's children on this earth and more than ever will commence there in all perfection and never end, is ruled by our Lord Jesus Christ Himself, the Lord of all lords and King of all kings and potentates, to whom alone the Father has given all power and has set Him only and Him alone at His right hand through Himself and His Holy Spirit. This kingdom, as Christ's kingdom (which is also called the Christian Church), has no earthly king, no worldly government, and no under-officer. The Lord Himself is king in His kingdom as well as the appointed head of the Church. He has not commended it to any other; He does not give His honor to another. His eternal realm, dominion, office and rule do not devolve upon any temporal dominion, kingdom or people and will never be destroyed, but it will at the last day grind to pieces and destroy all kingdoms of this world, but it will remain forever. Dan. 2 and 1 Cor. 15.

This king rules the souls and consciences by His word of grace, by His holy, eternal Gospel. There is no force nor duress there, but spiritual liberty and spontaneity. The Church of God is open. God lets everyone go in and out, Is. 60. There is no compulsion, war, or strife: it is a prototype of the building of Solomon's temple where no hammer-blow or violence was heard. There is love and harmony, grace, peace, and compassion among all His children, among the people of the Gospel and the New Testament. Of this the prophet Isaiah in particular, and the Holy Scripture of the New Testament, bear glorious witness. But thereby the service of the New Testament is in no wise annulled. However, the apostles and servants of Jesus Christ have received no other command from the Lord, but this, that they shall teach and testify of Him, proclaim the Gospel of the grace of God, invite everyone to Christ the Lord, preach repentance in His name, praise His glorious grace, make known to all the world the unspeakable benefit of His obedience and cross, and briefly, that they teach to know the Lord Christ aright, both according to the state of His cross and the state of His glory; that the office of forgiveness of sin, of the dispensation of the Holy Spirit, of regeneration and repentance, of grace and remission, etc., without any addition and mingling of all creatures or elements, be reserved in all respects for the Lord Christ, the regnant king. Such faithful servants of Christ who praise only His glory and point only to Him in all external worship, have no power but for the betterment of the Church of God. They do not teach to offend, drive out or kill anyone; they do not mingle the spiritual kingdom of Christ with the worldly, political kingdom as has been done by many in this time to great damage and ruin. . . .

Up to this point, liberal Christianity consisted of a number of disconnected heresies. There was no theological system, no popular movement; there were no churches, colleges, or territories that could be called Unitarian.

In the years after 1550 many of these isolated impulses were unified into two religious movements: the Unitarian church in Transylvania and the Minor Reformed Church in Poland. These constitute the highest achievements of organized Antitrinitarianism in the sixteenth century.

Transylvania, comprising the eastern tip of the old Kingdom of Hungary, was an independent country from 1543 to 1691. It is now a part of Romania. A land of hills and valleys, streams and woods, its name means "beyond the forest region" (of Hungary). Peopled by descendants of Magyar and Szekler settlers and a variety of other groups, the country was an ancient "melting pot," with cautious harmony and some intermarriage the prevailing order.

Nominally Catholic until the sixteenth century, Transylvania was converted to Protestantism between 1520, when the first Lutheran books and missionaries arrived, and 1556 when the government disestablished the Catholic Church. In 1561 John Sigismund (1540-1571) became King of Transylvania, the first and only Unitarian king in history. John was frail and artistic, an accomplished linguist and a superior monarch. Above all, he was deeply interested in religion, and sought to pacify the conflicts between Roman Catholics, Greek Orthodox, Lutherans, Calvinists, and Unitarians in his realm. His closest adviser was Dr. Giorgio Biandrata who had helped establish Antitrinitarianism in Poland. Out of personal conviction, therefore, and practical political considerations, he fostered a policy of open discussion and broad toleration of all viewpoints which made Transylvania the freest country in Europe in religious matters.

Transylvania's first decree of religious toleration came in 1557. It was renewed in 1563. Five years later, after the Diet had voted it unanimously with a request that John "declare and strengthen" the prior decrees, the young King issued this famous Act of Religious Tolerance and Freedom of Conscience.[5]

His Majesty, our Lord, in what manner he—together with his realm [i.e., the Diet]—legislated in the matter of religion at the previous Diets, in the same manner now, in this Diet, he reaffirms that in every place the preachers shall preach and explain the Gospel each according to his understanding of it, and if the congregation like it, well, if not, no one shall compel them for their souls would not be satisfied, but they shall be permitted to keep a preacher whose teaching they approve. Therefore none of the superintendents or others shall abuse the preachers, no one shall be reviled for his religion by anyone, according to the previous statutes, and it is not permitted that anyone should threaten anyone else by imprisonment or by removal from his post for his teaching, for faith is the gift of God, this comes from hearing, which hearing is by the word of God.

The great prophet and spokesperson of Transylvanian Unitarianism was Francis David (1510-1579). Trained for the Catholic priesthood, he became successively a Lutheran, a Calvinist, and a Unitarian. So marked was his ability that he was elected superintendent of each of the Protestant confessions in which he held membership! Indeed, for many years the Transylvanian Unitarians were referred to as "of Francis David's religion."

David was an incomparable public speaker—one who, as a contemporary said of him, "seemed to have the Old and New Testaments at his tongue's end." He had been influenced by the writings of Servetus, and was an advocate of freedom of belief with each individual accountable only to God. The religious situation was ripe for a person of his talents, for the Reformed church had not yet adopted a fixed doctrine and there was room to think freely.

In 1566, on the recommendation of Biandrata, King John appointed David his court preacher. As such David became spokesperson for the Unitarian party in the national debates called by the king to clarify religious issues of the time.

The major debates during John's reign were at Gyualafehervar (pronounced gyoo'-law-feh-hayr-var) in 1566 and 1568, and at Nagyvarad (nawdg'-vah-radw) in 1569. They attracted the same attention that American presidential nominating conventions attract now, for religion then was politics and was as important to the people as politics is today.

The first debate was inconclusive. The second, which immediately followed King John's decree of toleration, established Unitarianism as a popular faith and David as its champion. The third at Nagyvarad in 1569 was, in the judgment of one Hungarian historian, "the decisive debate" which produced the "final triumph of Unitarianism." Here are David's propositions which formed the basis of the debate.[6]

I. The Trinity held by the pope of Rome is really a belief in four or five Gods; one substance, God, three separate persons each of which are Gods, and one man, Christ. According to Francis

David God is only one, that Father from whom and by whom is everything, who is above everything, who created everything through the word of his wisdom and the breath of his mouth. Outside of this God there is no other God, neither three, neither four, neither in substance, neither in persons, because the Scripture nowhere teaches anything about a triple God.

II. One is the Son of God, Jesus Christ, God and man, of whom we cannot say either that he is first born or that he is the only begotten of God because such a person would not be both God and man.

III. The Scripture's God-son who was supposed to have been born of the substance of God from the beginning of eternity is nowhere mentioned, neither a God-son who would be the second person of the Trinity descended from heaven and become flesh. This is only human invention and superstition and as such is to be discarded.

IV. There is no other Son of God than the one who was begotten in the womb of the virgin by the Holy Spirit.

V. Jesus Christ is God and man but he did not create himself, the Father gave him his divinity, the Father had him begotten by the Holy Spirit, the Father sanctified him and sent him into the world.

VI. The equality of Christ with God is only of a kind which God gave him, God remaining in his divine sovereignty above everyone else.

VII. He [Francis David] does not deny that the Son of God was present in the eternal thought of God because there is no difference in time before God, for God everything is present tense; but the Scriptures nowhere teach that the Son of God would have been born from the beginning of eternity.

VIII. Christ is the Son of God, he was neither purely human nor purely God before the angel announced him to Mary and the shepherds; he was the Son of David in flesh, he was the Son of God in spirit, anointed high priest, judge and Lord above everyone else, he is our hope and fulfillment.

IX. The Holy Spirit is not self-created God, not a third person

in the Trinity, but the Spirit of the Father and of the Son, a seal
of inheritance, life-giving strength, which the Father realizes in us
through the Son, to be seen in ourselves and in our actions.

David summed up the debate afterward in these words: "I followed the line of Scripture but my opponents hid it in a bag, they
turned light into darkness when they made three of the Father God
and two of Christ. Their religion is self-contradictory to the extent that even they cannot present it in a whole. Nevertheless they
will see that even against their will God will prove his truth."

In 1571 Unitarianism reached its zenith of popularity with almost
five hundred congregations existing, and the Diet recognized it as
one of four "received" religions (i.e., those protected by law). However, King John died in the same year, and with his tolerant spirit
absent the Calvinists shortly condemned David for innovations and
curtailed the freedom of the Unitarians. David died in prison in
1579, a religious martyr and a national hero. His conviction that
"God is One!" has continued to burn in the hearts of Transylvanian
and Hungarian Unitarians down to the present day.

The name "Unitarian" itself is of Transylvanian origin, having
been first used there in the year 1600. Later, in the Agreement of
Dees in 1638, it was employed to designate the most liberal of the
four received religions. Scholars disagree concerning its derivation
—whether the word comes from the Unitarian belief in the unity of
God (in contrast to the term "Trinitarian"), or from the union
of the four Protestant churches under the Decree of Religious
Tolerance of 1568. In the eighteenth century the name came into
widespread usage, gradually superseding "Antitrinitarian" and "Socinian" in the popular religious vocabulary.

The Seventeenth Century: Socinianism, a Mature Heresy

In the seventeenth century, Antitrinitarianism was in large meas-ure channelled into a distinct doctrinal and ethical system—Socinianism, named for the Italian Antitrinitarians Laelius and Faustus Socinus. Its source was the kingdom of Poland, where it flourished for almost a century under sympathetic patrons and tolerant monarchs before being annihilated by Calvinist and Jesuit oppressions.

Socinianism exerted a powerful influence westward to Holland and England. Because of its doctrinal radicalism and revolutionary social views, the movement was deeply despised, but was heartily welcomed by those who were prepared to receive its good news.

Poland in the sixteenth century was the leading nation in eastern Europe. Several factors made it a hospitable ground for Protestant and Antitrinitarian teachings: a tradition of toleration of various religions—Roman Catholic, Greek Orthodox, Jewish, and Mohammedan; the weakness and corruption of the Roman Church; the liberalizing influence of the Italian Renaissance on Polish culture and court life; and the enthusiasm of many young nobles for Protestant doctrines absorbed at German universities.

The preaching of Peter Gonesius in 1556 sparked an Antitrinitarian movement within the Reformed (Calvinist) church. This Antitrinitarian movement became the Minor Reformed Church of Poland in 1563 when it separated from the parent body.

The Minor church's central doctrine was in opposition to the Trinity. Beyond this there was wide disagreement on such questions as the person of Christ, the worship of the Holy Spirit, and the function and timing of baptism. Its most notable social practice was that of love and tolerance in human relationships. The members, who called themselves the Polish Brethren, took Jesus' teachings so literally that they refused to bear arms and accept civil office; and at Racow they formed a Christian community governed according to the precepts in the Sermon on the Mount.

The smallest of the four Protestant churches, the Minor church numbered about one hundred congregations in 1579, when Faustus Socinus arrived in Poland.

More than any other person, Faustus Socinus (1539-1604), an Italian, was the architect of modern Unitarianism. In his thinking he carried his predecessors' ideas—notably those of his heretical uncle, Laelius—to their logical conclusions by asserting that Jesus was more human being than God. His treatise, On Jesus Christ the Savior, had argued that Jesus saved humans not by dying for them but by setting an example for them to follow. In his leadership of the Polish churches Socinus fostered a pattern of Scriptural fidelity, liturgical simplicity, and sympathetic administration.

In his published writings, Socinianism "swept from Poland in a tide" that was to cleanse Christian thinking all across Europe until the nineteenth century.

By far the most influential Socinian work was the Racovian Catechism, so-called because it was published at Racow, the Socinian capital. Socinus wrote the first draft and commissioned his friends to finish it. It was published in 1605 and widely translated and reprinted. Most catechisms are designed for the instruction of children or converts, but this catechism was, in the words of the historian Adolf Harnack, "a course of instruction for producing theologians." Essentially, it was a systematic statement of Socinian doctrine for propaganda purposes. It served well. Long after Socinus' death in 1604, after the Racow press was destroyed in 1638, and after the Socinians were forced by Jesuit oppression to flee Poland in 1660, the Racovian Catechism carried the gospel of Christian freedom to the world.[7]

OF THE HOLY SCRIPTURES

Question. I Would fain learn of you what the Christian Religion is.

Answer. The Christian Religion is the way of attaining eternall life, discovered by God.

Q. But where is it discovered?

A. In the holy Scriptures, especially that of the new Covenant [i.e., New Testament].

Q. Is there then any other Holy Scripture, besides that of the New Covenant?

A. Yes.

Q. What is it?

A. The writings of the old Covenant [i.e., Old Testament]. . . .

CHAP. II TOUCHING THE SUFFICIENCY OF THE HOLY SCRIPTURES

Q. That the sacred Scriptures are firm and certain, you have sufficiently proved, I would therefore further learn, whether they be so sufficient, as that in things necessary to eternall life we ought to rest in them only?

A. They are altogether sufficient for that, inasmuch as Faith on the Lord Jesus Christ, and obedience to his Commandements, (which twain are the requisites of eternall life) are sufficiently delivered and explained in the Scripture of the very New Covenant.

Q. If it be so, then what need is there of Traditions, which the Church of Rome holdeth to be necessary unto eternall life, calling them the unwritten Scripture?

A. You rightly gather, that they are unnecessary to eternall life.

Q. What then must we think of them?

A. Not only that they were fancied and invented without just cause and necessity, but also to the great hazard of the Christian Faith.

Q. What may that hazard be?

A. Because those Traditions give men an occasion of turning aside from divine Truth to falshood, and the imaginations of men.

Q. But they seem to assert those Traditions from the very Scripture.

A. Those testimonies which they produce out of the Scripture to assert those Traditions, do indeed demonstrate that Christ and the Apostles spake and did certain things which are not comprehended in the holy Scriptures, but no ways prove that they were delivered from hand to hand by them to be perpetually so conserved, or that those things which are consigned in the holy Scripture, are not sufficient to Religion and salvation. . . .

OF THE KNOWLEDGE OF CHRIST
CHAP. I TOUCHING THE PERSON OF CHRIST

Q. Inasmuch as you have said that those things have been discovered by Jesus Christ, that concern the will of God as it properly belongeth unto them, who shall obtain eternall life, I would entreat

you to declare those things to me concerning Jesus Christ, which
are needfull to be known.

A. I am content. First therefore you must know that those things
partly concern the Essence, partly the Office of Jesus Christ.

Q. What are the things that concern his Essence or Person?

A. Only that he is a true man by nature, as the holy Scriptures
frequently testifie concerning that matter, and namely, I Tim. 2. 5.
There is one Mediator of God and men, the man Christ Jesus. And
I Cor. 15. 21. Since by man came death, by man also came the
Resurrection from the dead. And indeed such a one God heretofore
promised by the Prophets, and such a one the Apostles Creed, acknowledged by all Christians, confesseth Jesus Christ to be.

Q. Is the Lord Jesus then a meer man?

A. By no means. For he was conceived of the Holy Spirit, and
born of the Virgin Mary, and therefore is from his very conception
and birth the Son of God, as we read, Luke 1. 35. where the Angell
thus speaketh to the Virgin Mary, The Holy Spirit shall come upon
thee, and the power of the Highest shall overshadow thee, therefore
also that Holy Thing Generated shall be called the Son of God.
That I may omit other causes, which you shall afterwards discover
in the Person of Jesus Christ, and most evidently shew, that the
Lord Jesus ought by no means to be reputed a meer man.

Q. You said a little before that the Lord Jesus is a man by nature,
hath he not also a divine Nature?

A. At no hand; for that is repugnant not onely to sound Reason,
but also to the holy Scriptures.

Q. Shew me how it is repugnant to sound Reason.

A. First, because two substances indued with opposite properties,
cannot combine into one Person, and such properties are mortality
and immortality; to have beginning, and to be without beginning; to
be mutable, and immutable. Again, two Natures, each whereof is
apt to constitute a severall person, cannot be huddled into one
Person. For instead of one, .there must of necessity arise two persons, & consequently become two Christs, whom all men without
controversie acknowledge to be one, and his Person one.

Q. But when they alledge that Christ is so constituted of a
divine and humane Nature, as a man is of a body and soul, what
answer must we make to them?

A. That in this case there is a wide difference; for they say that the two Natures in Christ are so united that Christ is both God and Man. Whereas the soul and body in a man are so conjoyned, as that a man is neither soul nor body. For neither doth the soul nor the body severally constitute a Person. But as the divine Nature doth by it self constitute a Person, so must the humane by it self of necessity also constitute.

Q. Shew how it is also repugnant to the Scripture that Christ should have a divine Nature.

A. First, because the Scripture proposeth to us but one God by nature, whom we formerly demonstrated to be the Father of Christ. Secondly, the same Scripture witnesseth that Jesus Christ is a man by nature, as was formerly shewn. Thirdly, because whatsoever divine excellency Christ hath, the Scripture testifieth that he hath it by gift of the Father. John 3. 35. John 5. 19, 20, 21, 22, 23, 26, 27. John 10. 25. John 13. 3. John 14. 10. Acts 2. 33. Rev. 2. 26, 27. 2 Pet. 1. 17. Finally, because the Scripture doth most evidently shew, that Jesus Christ doth perpetually ascribe all his Divine acts not to himself, or any Divine nature of his own, but to the Father; who seeth not that such a Divine nature as the Adversaries imagine in Christ, would have been altogether idle, and of no use? . . .

Q. I perceive that Christ hath not a divine nature, but is a true man, now tell me of what avail unto salvation the knowledge hereof will be?

A. From the knowledge of this, that Christ is a true man, a sure and well grounded confirmation of our hope doth follow, which by the contrary opinion is exceedingly shaken, and almost taken away.

Q. How so?

A. Because it followeth from the adverse opinion, that Christ is not a true man, for since they deny that there is in Christ the person of a man, who seeth that they with one and the same labour deny him to be a true man, in that he cannot be a true man, who wanteth the person of a man, but if Christ had not been a true man, he could not die, and consequently not rise again from the dead, whereby our hope which resteth on the resurrection of Christ, as on a firm basis, and foundation, may be easily shaken, and well nigh thrown down, but that opinion, which acknowledgeth Christ to be a true man, who conversing in the world, was obedient to the Father, even unto death, doth assert, and clearly determine that the same died, and was by God raised from the dead, and indued with immortality, and so in a wonderful manner, supporteth, and proppeth, our hope concerning eternall life, setting before our eyes the very image of that thing, and assuring us thereby, as it were with a pledge, that we also though we be mortall and die; shall notwithstanding in due time rise from death, to come into the society of the same blessed immortality, whereof he is made partaker if we tread in his steps. . . .

CHAP. VII   TOUCHING THE CONFIRMATION OF THE DIVINE WILL

Q. How Jesus declared unto us the Divine Will, hath been explained, I would now have it also explained how he confirmed the same?

A. There are three things of Christ that did confirme the Divine Will which he declared; first, the absolute innocency of his life, John 8. 46. I John 3. 5. Secondly, his great, and innumerable Miracles, John 15. 24. John 21. 25. Thirdly, his death, I Tim. 2. 6. chap. 6. 13. All these three are united in that noted place of John, I Epist. 5. 8. There are three that bare record on Earth, The Spirit, the Water, and the Bloud. For by the Spirit, without question the holy Spirit is meant, by whose Vertue the Miracles of Christ were wrought, Acts 10. 38. As by Water is understood the Purity of his life, and by Bloud, his Bloudy death.

Q. What was the Innocency of Christs Life, and how was the Will of God confirmed thereby?

A. The Innocency of his Life was such, that he not onely committed no sin, neither was guil found in his mouth, nor could he be convicted of any crime, but he lived so transcendently pure, as that none, either before, or after, did equallize him, so that he came next to God himself in Holiness, and was therein very like to him. Whence it followeth, that the Doctrine delivered by him was most true.

Q. What were his Miracles, and how did they confirm the Divine Will?

A. The Miracles were so great, as none before him ever did; and so many, as that had they been set down in particular, the world would not contain the Books. And these Miracles do therefore make to the confirming of the will of God, in that it is not imaginable that God would invest any one with such power, as was truly Divine, who had not been sent by him.

CHAP. VIII OF CHRISTS DEATH

Q. What was the Death of Christ, and how did it confirm the Will of God?

A. Such a death, as had all sorts of afflictions ushering it in, and was of it self most bitter and ignominious, so that the Scripture thereupon testifieth that he was made like to his brethren in all things, Heb. 2. 17. . . .

The 1614 Latin edition of the Racovian Catechism was dedicated to King James I of England. Rather than being flattered or won to its teachings, he ordered it burned as a work of Satan. But this was neither the beginning nor the end of Antitrinitarianism in England. Antitrinitarian ideas had arisen spontaneously as early as the fifteenth century. They increased with the influx of several thousand Protestant refugees from the Continent in the 1530's and 1540's. British scholars and travellers conversed with Polish and Transylvanian Antitrinitarians in Holland. Beginning about 1590 Socinian books from the Racow press, many of them translated and reprinted in Holland, quietly filtered into England to be passed from hand to hand and discussed in secret.

The first effective advocate of Unitarianism in England was John Biddle (1615-1662), a young schoolteacher who spent half his adult life in prison as the victim of medieval heresy laws and overzealous ecclesiastics. In 1644 Biddle composed a brief theological statement for his friends. His purpose was to establish the unity of God by showing from Scripture that the Holy Spirit is not God but only a manifestation of God. Published three years later in 1647, it was titled XII Arguments Drawn Out of the Scripture: Wherein the commonly received Opinion touching the Deity of the Holy Spirit, is clearly and fully refuted.[8] Two of the twelve arguments are given here.

ARGUMENT I

He that is distinguished from God, is not God. The Holy Spirit is distinguished from God. Ergo [the Holy Spirit is not God].

The Major is evident: for if he should be both God, and distinguished from himself; which implies a contradiction. The Minor is confirmed by the whole current of the Scripture, which calleth him the Spirit of God, and faith that he is sent by God, and searcheth the depths of God, &c. Neither let any Man here think to fly to that ignorant Refuge of making a distinction between the Essence and Person of God, saying that the Holy Spirit is distinguished from God, taken Personally, not Essentially: For this wretched distinction (to omit the mention of the Primitive Fathers) is not only unheard of in Scripture, and so to be rejected, it being Presumption to affirm any thing of the unsearchable Nature of God, which he hath not first affirmed of himself in the Scripture; but is also disclaimed by Reason. For first, it is impossible for any Man, if he would but endeavor to conceive the thing, and not delude both himself and others with empty Terms and Words without understanding, to distinguish the Person from the Essence of God, and not to frame two Beings or Things in his Mind, and consequently two Gods. Secondly, If the Person be distinct from the Essence of God, then it must needs be something; since nothing hath no Accident, and therefore neither can it happen to it to be distinguished. If something, then either some finite or infinite thing: if finite, then there will be something finite in God, and consequently, since by the Confession of the Adversaries everything in God is God himself, God will be Finite; which the Adversaries themselves will likewise confess to be absurd. If Infinite, then there will be two Infinites in God, to wit, the Person and Essence of God, and consequently two Gods; which is more absurd than the former. Thirdly, To talk of God taken impersonally, is ridiculous, not only because there is no Example thereof in Scripture, but because God is the Name of a Person, and signifieth him that hath sublime Dominion or Power; and when it is put for the most High God, it denoteth him who with Soveraign and Absolute Authority ruleth over all; but none but a Person can rule over others, all Actions being proper to Persons; wherefore to take God otherwise than personally is to take him otherwise than he is, and indeed to mistake him.

ARGUMENT VIII

He that changeth place, is not God. The Holy Spirit changeth place. Ergo.

The Major is plain: for if God should change place, he would cease to be where he was before, and begin to be where he was not before; which everteth his Omnipresence, and consequently, by the Confession of the Adversaries themselves, his Deity. The Minor is ocularly apparent, if following the Advice of the Adversaries, you will but go to Jordan; for there you shall have the Holy Spirit in a bodily Shape descending from Heaven, which is the terminus a quo; and alighting upon Christ, which is the terminus ad quam, Luk 3. 21, 22, Joh 1. 32. Neither let any Man alledge, that as much is spoken of God, Exod. 3. and Chap. 20. and Gen. 18. For if you compare Acts 7. 30, 35, 38, 53. Gal. 3. 19. Heb. 2. 2, 3, and Chap. 13. 2. with the foresaid places, you shall find, that it was not God himself that came down, but only an Angel, sustaining the Person and Name of God; which hath no place in the History: touching the descent of the Holy Spirit.

Stung by the XII Arguments and fearful of rampant heresy, Parliament the next year voted the death penalty to deniers of the Trinity. Biddle, in true Servetus fashion, responded by publishing his version of the Trinity based on Scripture and implying that everybody else's was false. His Confession of Faith touching the Holy Trinity (1648)[9] shows strong Socinian parallels, especially in the assertion that Jesus "hath no other than a human nature." When out of prison Biddle met weekly with his followers. But the magistrates, goaded by the Presbyterian guardians of orthodoxy, would allow him no peace. He died in 1662, the foremost progenitor of English Unitarianism.

ARTICLE I. I believe, that there is one most High God, Creator of Heaven and Earth, and first Cause of all things pertaining to our Salvation, and consequently the ultimate Object of our Faith and Worship; and that this God is none but the Father of our Lord Jesus Christ, the first Person of the HOLY TRINITY. [Exegesis follows each of the articles.]

ARTICLE II. I believe, That there is one chief Son of the most High God, or Spiritual, Heavenly, and perpetual Lord and King, set over the Church by God, and Second Cause of all Things pertaining to our Salvation, and consequently, the intermediate Object of our

Faith and Worship: and this Son of the most High God is none but Jesus Christ, the second person of the HOLY TRINITY.

ARTICLE III. I believe, That Jesus Christ, to the intent he might be our Brother, and have a Fellow-feeling of our Infirmaties, and so become the more ready to help us, (the consideration whereof, is the greatest Encouragement to Piety that can be imagined) hath no other than a Human Nature, and therefore in this very Nature is not only a Person (since none but a Human Person can be our Brother) but also our Lord, yea our God.

ARTICLE IV. Whence, though he be our God, by reason of his Divine Sovereignty over us, and Worship due to such Sovereignty, yet he is not the most high God, the same with the Father, but subordinate to him.

ARTICLE V. Again; Though he be a God, subordinate to the most High God, as having received his Godhead, and whatsoever he hath, from the Father; yet may not anyone thence rightly infer, that by this Account there will be another God, or two Gods? For though we may, with allowance of the Scripture, say, that there are many Gods, yet neither will the Scripture, nor the thing it self permit us to say, that there is another God, or two Gods: because when a word in its own nature common to many, hath been appropriated, and ascribed to one by way of Excellency, (as that of God hath been to the Father:) albeit this doth not hinder us from saying, that there are many of that Name; yet doth it from saying, that there is another, or two, since that would be all one as if we should say, that there is another, or two most Excellent, (which is absurd:) for when two are segregated in this manner out of many, they claim Excellency to themselves alike. Thus though some faithful Man be a Son of God, subordinate to the chief Son of God Christ Jesus, yet may we not thereupon say, that there is another Son of God, or two Sons of God, (since that would be to make another, or two Sons of God by way of Excellency, whereas there can be but one such a Son) howbeit otherwise the Scripture warrents us to say, that there are many Sons of God.

ARTICLE VI. I Believe that there is one principle Minister of God and Christ, peculiarly sent from Heaven to sanctify the Church, who, by reason of his eminency and intimacy with God, is singled out of the number of the other Heavenly Ministers or Angels, and comprised in the Holy TRINITY, being the Third Person thereof; and that this Minister of God and Christ is the Holy Spirit.

In the year of Biddle's death, Parliament outlawed all non-Episcopal worship and clergy in the Act of Uniformity (1662) which remained in force until the Toleration Act of 1689. As always, however, oppression spawned unrest, and Antitrinitarianism spread rapidly. Biddle's tracts were widely circulated in England and Holland (where they nourished the Remonstrant and Arminian movements). Large numbers of Socinian books penetrated the churches, the universities, and even Parliament itself. The summit of the liberal spirit was probably the mind of John Milton, whose Antitrinitarian Treatise on Christian Doctrine was completed shortly before the great poet's death in 1674. (Lost among his papers for a century and a half, its discovery and publication in 1823 dramatically confirmed Milton's theological unorthodoxy.) Free-floating Antitrinitarianism in the Church of England produced the celebrated Trinitarian Controversy for a decade after 1687.

In 1685 the English philosopher John Locke (1632-1704) addressed to a friend, in Latin, "A Letter Concerning Toleration." It was composed in Holland, where Locke had sought refuge from the stifling religious atmosphere at home, and published in England in 1689. Coupled with the Toleration Act of 1689, Locke's letter— and those which followed it—effected a deep and permanent change in English attitudes toward church and state, the proper role of clergy in matters of belief, and the rights of religious minorities.[10]

Honored Sir,

Since you are pleased to enquire what are my thoughts about the mutual toleration of Christians in their different professions of religion, I must needs answer you freely, that I esteem that toleration to be the chief characteristical mark of the true Church. For whatsoever some people boast of the antiquity of places and names, or of the pomp of their outward worship; others, of the reformation of their discipline; all, of the orthodoxy of their faith; (for every one is orthodox to himself:) these things, and all others of this nature, are much rather marks of men striving for power and empire over one another, than of the Church of Christ. Let any one have never so true a claim to all these things, yet if he be destitute of charity, meekness, and good-will in general towards all mankind, even to those that are not Christians, he is certainly yet short of being a true Christian himself. "The kings of the Gentiles exercise Lordship over them," said our Savior to his disciples, "but ye shall not be so" (Luke 22. 25). The business of true religion is quite another thing. It is not instituted in order to the erecting of an external pomp, nor to the obtaining of ecclesiastical dominion, nor to the exercising of compulsive force; but to the regulating of mens lives according to the rules of virtue and piety. Whosoever will list himself under the banner of Christ, must in the first place, and above all things, make war upon his own lusts and vices. It is in vain for any man to usurp the name of Christian, without holiness of life, purity of manners, and benignity and meekness of spirit. . . . It would indeed be very hard for one that appears careless about his own salvation, to persuade me that he were extremely concern'd for mine. For it is impossible that those should sincerely and heartily apply themselves to make other people Christians, who have not really embraced the Christian religion in their own hearts. If the Gospel and the Apostles may be credited, no man can be a Christian without charity, and without that faith which works, not by force, but by love. . . .

I esteem it above all things necessary to distinguish exactly the business of civil government from that of religion, and to settle the just bounds that lie between the one and the other. . . . It is the duty of the civil magistrate, by the impartial execution of equal laws, to secure unto all the people in general, and to every one of his subjects in particular, the just possession of these things belonging to this life. . . . Now that the whole jurisdiction of the magistrate reaches only to these civil concernments; and that all civil power, right and dominion, is bounded and confined to the only care of promoting these things; and that it neither can nor ought in any manner to be extended to the salvation of souls, these following considerations seem unto me abundantly to demonstrate.

First, because the care of souls is not committed to the civil magistrate, any more than to other men. It is not committed unto him, I say, by God; because it appears not that God has ever given any such authority to one man over another, as to compel any one to his religion. Nor can any such power be vested in the magistrate by the consent of the people; because no man can so far abandon the care of his own salvation, as blindly to leave it to the choice of any other. . . .

In the second place. The care of souls cannot belong to the civil magistrate, because his power consists only in outward force; but true and saving religion consists in the inward persuasion of the mind, without which nothing can be acceptable to God. And such is the nature of the Understanding, that it cannot be compell'd to the belief of any thing by outward force. Confiscation of estate, imprisonment, torments, nothing of that nature can have any such efficacy as to make men change the inward judgment that they have framed of things. . . .

These considerations . . . seem unto me sufficient to conclude that all the power of civil government relates only to mens civil interests, is confined to the care of the things of this world, and hath nothing to do with the world to come.

But after all, the principal consideration, and which absolutely determines this controversy, is this. Although the magistrate's opinion in religion be sound, and the way that he appoints be truly evangelical, yet if I be not thoroughly persuaded thereof in my own mind, there will be no safety for me in following it. No way whatsoever that I shall walk in against the dictates of my conscience, will ever bring me to the mansions of the blessed. I may grow rich by art that I take not delight in; I may be cured of some disease by remedies that I have not faith in; but I cannot be saved by a religion that I distrust, and by a worship that I abhor. . . . Faith only, and inward sincerity, are the things that procure acceptance with God. The most likely and most approved remedy can have no effect upon the patient, if his stomach reject it as soon as taken. And you will in vain cram a medicine down a sick man's throat, which his particular constitution will be sure to turn into poison. In a word. Whatsoever may be doubtful in religion, yet this at least is certain, that no religion, which I believe not to be true, can be either true, or profitable unto me. In vain therefore do princes compel their subjects to come into their church-communion, under pretence of saving their souls. If they believe, they will come of their own accord; if they believe not, their coming will nothing avail them. . . .

It is not the diversity of opinions, (which cannot be avoided) but the refusal of toleration to those that are of different opinions, (which might have been granted) that has produced all the bustles and wars, that have been in the Christian world, upon account of religion. The heads and leaders of the Church, moved by avarice and insatiable desire for dominion, making use of the immoderate ambition of magistrates, and the credulous superstition of the giddy multitude, have incensed and animated them against those that dissent from themselves; by preaching unto them, contrary to the laws of the Gospel, and to the precepts of charity, that schismatics and heretics are to be outed of their possessions, and destroyed. And they have mixed together, and confounded two things, that are in themselves most different, the Church and the Common-wealth. . . . God almighty grant, I beseech him, that the Gospel of Peace may at length be preached, and that civil magistrates growing more careful to conform their own consciences to the law of God, and less solicitous about the binding of other mens consciences by human laws, may like fathers of their country, direct all their counsel and endeavors to promote universally the civil welfare of all their children; except only of such as are arrogant, ungovernable, and injurious to their brethren; and that all ecclesiastical men, who boast themselves to be the successors of the Apostles, walking peaceably and modestly in the Apostles' steps, without intermedling with State-affairs, may apply themselves wholly to promote the salvation of souls.

Although Locke remained in the Church of England all his life, his religious thinking was radical. His library contained the writings of Castellio, Socinus, Biddle, the Racovian Catechism, and most of the influential Socinians. He believed in a simple, reasonable, benevolent Christianity based on the Bible and especially on the moral teachings of Jesus. For him, Scripture showed a clear way to eternal life led by Christ, "the Captain of our salvation."

When, therefore, the leading churchmen abandoned Christian truth for subtle speculations and rancorous hair-splitting during the Trinitarian Controversy, the cause of religion suffered in his eyes. In an attempt to restate its essential doctrines, Locke in 1695 anonymously published a treatise on The Reasonableness of Christianity. One minister called it "one of the best books that have been published for at least these sixteen hundred years." Appearing at the

*height of the Trinitarian Controversy, it strengthened the liberal
cause and placed Locke, the leading philosopher of his time, in the
same camp theologically with the Socinians and Unitarians.*[11]

Though the works of Nature, in every part of them, sufficiently
evidence a Deity; yet the world made so little use of their Reason,
that they saw him not, where even by the impressions of himself he
was easy to be found. Sense and lust blinded their minds in some,
and a careless inadvertency in others, and fearful apprehensions in
most (who either believed there were, or could not but suspect
there might be, superior unknown Beings) gave them up into the
hands of their priests, to fill their heads with false notions of the
Deity, and their worship with foolish rites, as they pleased: and
what dread or craft once began, devotion soon made sacred, and
religion immutable. In this state of darkness and ignorance of the
true God, vice and superstition held the world. Nor could any help
be had, or hoped for from Reason; which could not be heard, and
was judged to have nothing to do in the case: the priests, every
where, to secure their Empire, having excluded Reason from having
any thing to do in religion. And in the crowd of wrong notions, and
invented rites, the world had almost lost the sight of the one only
true God. The rational and thinking part of mankind, 'tis true,
when they sought after him, found the one supreme, invisible God:
but if they acknowledged and worshipped him, it was only in their
own minds. They kept this truth locked up in their own breasts as
a secret, nor ever dared venture it amongst the people, much less
amongst the priests, those wary guardians of their own creeds and
profitable inventions. Hence we see that Reason, speaking never so
clearly to the wise and virtuous, had never authority enough to prevail on the multitude, and to persuade the societies of men, that
there was but one God, that alone was to be owned and worshipped.
The belief and worship of one God, was the national religion of the
Israelites alone: and if we will consider it, it was introduced and
supported amongst the people by Revelation. They were in Goshen,
and had light, whilst the rest of the world were in almost Egyptian
darkness, without God in the world. . . .

In this state of darkness and error, in reference to the True God,
our Saviour found the world. But the clear Revelation he brought
with him, dissipated this darkness; made the One Invisible True

God known to the world: and that with such evidence and energy, that Polytheism and Idolatry hath no where been able to withstand it: but wherever the preaching of the truth he delivered, and the light of the Gospel hath come, those mists have been dispelled. And in effect we see that since our Savior's time, the Belief of One God has prevailed and spread it self over the face of the Earth. . . .

God out of the infiniteness of his mercy, has dealt with man as a compassionate and tender Father. He gave him Reason, and with it a Law: that could not be otherwise than what Reason should dictate; unless we should think, that a reasonable Creature should have an unreasonable Law. But considering the frailty of man, apt to run into corruption and misery, he promised a Deliverer, whom in his good time he sent; and then declared to all mankind, that whoever would believe him to be the Savior promised, and take him now raised from the dead, and constituted the Lord and Judge of all men, to be their king and ruler, should be saved. This is a plain intelligible proposition; and the all-merciful God seems herein to have consulted the poor of this world, and the bulk of mankind. These are articles that the laboring and illiterate man may comprehend. This is a religion suited to vulgar capacities; and the state of mankind in this world, destined to labor and travail. The writers and wranglers in religion fill it with niceties, and dress it up with notions, which they make necessary and fundamental parts of it; as if there were no way into the Church, but through the Academy or Lyceum. The greatest part of mankind have not leisure for learning and logic, and superfine distinctions from the schools. Where the hand is used to the plough and the spade, the head is seldom elevated to sublime notions, or exercised in mysterious reasoning. 'Tis well if men of that rank (to say nothing of the other sex) can comprehend plain propositions, and a short reasoning about things familiar to their minds, and nearly allied to their daily experience. Go beyond this, and you amaze the greatest part of mankind: and may as well talk Arabic to a poor day laborer, as the notions and language that the books and disputes of religion are filled with; and as soon you will be understood. . . . Had God intended that none but the learned scribe, the disputer or wise of this world, should be Christians, or be saved, thus religion should have been prepared for them, filled with speculations and niceties, obscure terms and abstract notions. But men of that expectation, men furnished with such acquisitions, the

Apostle tells us, I. Cor. i. are rather shut out from the simplicity of the Gospel; to make way for those poor, ignorant, illiterate, who heard and believed promises of a Deliverer, and believed Jesus to be him; who could conceive of a man dead and made alive again, and believe that he should at the end of the world, come again and pass sentence on all men, according to their deeds. That the poor had the Gospel preached to them; Christ makes a mark as well as business of his mission, Mat. xi. 5. And if the poor had the Gospel preached to them, it was, without doubt, such a Gospel as the poor could understand, plain and intelligible: and so it was, as we have seen, in the preachings of Christ and his Apostles.

The Eighteenth Century: Toward a New Principle of Authority

The dominant tensions in eighteenth-century Unitarianism centered on two problems: the relationship of dissent to the Established Church, and the role of reason in revealed religion. Fundamentally they were two aspects of the same problem—that of authority. As evidenced by the doctrinal turmoils of the Church of England and the legal entanglements of the Dissenters, the challenge to religious authority in England during the century was explicit and direct. By contrast, conditions in New England made for a slow shift of doctrine without outward schism. Thus the challenge to religious authority in America was more implicit and indirect. The break from orthodoxy in New England was not to come until the first quarter of the nineteenth century.

Eighteenth-century religious liberalism evolved simultaneously on both sides of the Atlantic. Its leaders corresponded voluminously, upholding and enlarging each other's views. By the end of the century, communication was supplemented by personal contact in the movements of Franklin and Jefferson to Europe and of Murray and Priestley to America. Doctrine also moved—from Emlyn's studious Antitrinitarianism to Lindsey's bold humanism, from Chauncy's half-humorous lamentations to Jefferson's scathing rationalism, from Christ-centered Socinianism to human-centered Unitarianism.

The word "Unitarian" first appeared on the title page of a book in 1687 in Stephen Nye's Brief History of the Unitarians. Nye was also the editor of several "Unitarian tracts" which opened up the issues between liberals and the orthodox after 1691. So compelling was the Unitarian position that in 1689 the Commissioners of the Church of England seriously considered omitting the Athanasian Creed from the Book of Common Prayer; it was this creed that the Socinians and Unitarians rejected as contrary to both Scripture and reason.

By the end of the seventeenth century, the Unitarians were shifting their attacks from the divinity of the Holy Spirit to the divinity of Christ—was Jesus God or not? In the Church of England the controversy over Christ's divinity was called the Arian controversy. (Arius was a fourth-century Catholic priest who held that Christ was of different substance from God, and therefore inferior to Him, although still a divine being. His view was declared heretical at the Council of Nicea in 325.)

The first important Arian work to appear in England was Thomas Emlyn's An Humble Inquiry into the Scripture Account of Jesus Christ (1702).[12] Emlyn (1663-1741) was a Presbyterian minister in Dublin, Ireland. After some years, a parishioner, observing that he never mentioned the Trinity, became suspicious and accused him of heresy. Emlyn acknowledged that he believed in "the God above all Gods" and soon published his Humble Inquiry to defend his views. His prooftext was Jesus' statement in John 14. 28, "The Father is greater than I." Emlyn sought to establish Jesus as a mediator between humankind and God, thus subtly to separate Jesus from God and in so doing to demolish the idea of the Trinity. He was immediately arrested and found guilty "of writing and publishing an infamous and scandalous libel declaring that Jesus Christ is not the Supreme God." Emlyn was the last Dissenter to suffer imprisonment for denying the Trinity.

That the Blessed Jesus has the Title of God ascribed sometimes to him in the holy Scriptures, is not denied by Arians or Socinians; but it remains to be examined in what Sense that Character, as given to him, is intended. Nor is this an unreasonable or needless Inquiry, since it is beyond all reasonable denial, that the Title of God is given in very different Senses in the Scripture.

(1) Sometimes it signifies the most High, Perfect and Infinite Being, who is of Himself alone, and owes neither his Being nor Authority, nor any thing to another: and this is what is most commonly intended, when we speak of God in ordinary Discourse, and in Prayer and Praise; we mean it of God in the most eminent Sense.

(2) At other times it has a lower Sense, and is made the Character of Persons who are invested with subordinate Authority and Power from that Supreme Being. Thus Angels are styled Gods, Psal. 8. 5. Thou hast made him a little lower than the Gods, as 'tis in the Margin: So Magistrates are Gods, Exod. 22. 28. Psal. 82. 1. John 10. 34,

35. And sometimes in the singular number, one Person is styled God, as Moses is twice so called, a God to Aaron, and afterwards a God to Pharaoh: and thus the Devil is called the God of this World, i.e. the Prince and mighty Ruler of it; tho by unjust Usurpation, and God's Permission. Now as he who alone is God, in the former sense, is infinitely above all these; so we find him distinguish'd from all others who are called God, by this Character, viz. a God of Gods, or the Chief of all Gods, with whom none of those Gods may be compared. So Philo describes him, to be not only the God of Men, but the God of Gods also. This is the highest and most glorious Epithet given him in the Old Testament, when it is designed to make a most magnificent mention of his peerless Greatness and Glory. . . .

Now the Question to be resolved is, in which of these two senses Christ is said to be God in the holy Scriptures? The bare Character of God determines nothing in this case, because it belongs both to the supreme and to subordinate Beings in Power and Authority: but the Question is, Whether Jesus Christ be the God of Gods, or above all Gods?

He is indeed the Lord of Lords; but that notes an inferior Character, compared with that of God of Gods, as appears by I Cor. 8. 5. tho it be included in the Superior; so that he who is above all Gods, is also over all Lords, but not contrariwise. In short, has Jesus Christ any God over him, who has greater Authority, and greater Ability than himself, or not? This will decide the matter: for if he have a God above him, then is he not the absolutely Supreme God, tho in relation to created Beings, he may be a God (or Ruler) over all.

Nor can we more clearly demonstrate this Point, than by showing, First, That Jesus Christ expressly speaks of another God than himself. Secondly, That he owns this God to be above or over himself. Thirdly, That he wants [i.e., lacks] those supereminent and infinite Perfections, which belong only to the Lord God of Gods. Of these I shall treat in a manner suited to vulgar Capacities; for I judge it very unfit to speak or write of important Articles (which the common People must believe, and must so far understand) in such a manner as leaves them wholly unintelligible.

First, Our Lord Jesus Christ expressly speaks of another God distinct from himself: several times we find him saying, My God, of another, Mat. 27. 46. My God, my God, why hast thou forsaken me? So John 20. 17 sure he intended not to say, My Self, my Self, why hast thou forsaken me? This God then was distinct from himself, as he declares in other places: He shall know my Doctrine, whether it be of God, or whether I speak of myself. So John 8. 42. where 'tis to be noted that he does not distinguish himself from him, as the Father, but as God; and therefore, in all just construction, he cannot be supposed to be that self-same God, from whom he distinguishes, and to whom he opposeth himself. . . .

Secondly, Our Lord Jesus owns, not only another than himself to be God; but also that he is above or over himself, which is plainly intimated also by his Apostles. Himself loudly proclaims his Subjection to the Father in many Instances; in general, he declares his Father to be greater than he: he says, he came not in his own, but his Father's Name or Authority; that he sought not his own, but God's Glory, nor made his own Will, but God's, his Rule; and in such a posture of Subjection he came down from Heaven into this Earth: so that it should seem, that Nature which did pre-exist, did not possess the Supreme Will, even before it was incarnate. Again, he owns his Dependence upon his God and Father, even for those things which it is pretended belong to him as God, viz. the Power of working Miracles, of raising the Dead, of executing universal Judgment; of all which he says, Of my own self I can do nothing.

Thirdly, That our blessed Lord Jesus disclaims those infinite Perfections which belong only to the Supreme God of Gods. And 'tis most certain, that if he want one, or any of these Perfections that are essential to the Deity, he is not God in the chief Sense: and if we find him disclaiming the one, he cannot challenge the other; for to deny himself to have all divine Perfections, or to deny himself to be the Infinite God, is the same thing. Let us, observe some Instances for the proof of this Point.

(1) One great and peculiar Perfection of the Deity, is absolute, underived Omnipotence: He who cannot work all Miracles, and do whatever he list of himself, without help from another can never be the Supreme Being, or God; because he appears to be an imperfect defective Being, comparatively, since he needs Help, and can receive additional Strength from another than himself.

Now it is most evident, that our Lord Jesus (whatever Power he had) confesses again and again, that he had not infinite Power of himself; Of myself I can do nothing. He had been speaking of great

Miracles, viz. raising the Dead, and executing all Judgment; but all
along takes care, Men shou'd know that his Sufficiency for these
things was of God the Father. In the beginning of the Discourse,
he says, The Son can do nothing but what he sees the Father do: so
in the middle, The Father has given to the Son to have Life in
himself: and as if he cou'd never too much inculcate this great Truth,
he adds towards the Conclusion, I can do nothing of myself, or,
from nothing that is my self do I draw this Power and Authority.
Sure this is not the Voice of God, but of a Man! For the most High
can receive from none; he cannot be made more Mighty or Wise,
because to absolute Perfection can be no Addition. And since Power
in God, is an essential Perfection; it follows, that if it be derived,
then so is the Essence or Being itself: which is Blasphemy against
the most High, for 'tis to Ungod Him; to number him among de-
pendent derivative Beings; whilst the Supreme God indeed is only
he who is the first Cause, and absolute Original of all. . . .

For my own part, as I write this under the serious Impressions of
those great Relations in which the blessed Jesus stands to me, whom
I credit as my great Teacher; whom I desire to admire and love as
my gracious endeared Benefactor, beyond Father and Mother, or
Friends, whom I reverence as my Lord and Ruler, and solemnly
expect as my final glorious Judge, who is to come in his own, and
in his Father's Glory; and in the mean time deal with God thro'
him, as my only Meditator, and Intercessor: so I earnestly profess,
that 'tis not without grievous and bitter Resentments, that I should
be employ'd in writing Things, which by so many well-meaning
Christians will be misinterpreted, to be derogatory to the Honour
of this great Redeemer. But I know he loves nothing but Truth in
his Cause, and will never be offended, I hope, with any who stand
by his own Words, viz. The Father is greater than I [John 14. 28].
I think it a dangerous thing to say God is not greater than he, or
is not the Head of Christ; for, whom will ye equal to me, saith the
Holy One? I am persuaded 'tis Truth I plead for, and that supports me.

Ten years later, in the Church of England, muffled unrest over the
divinity of Christ exploded with the publication of Samuel Clarke's
Scripture-Doctrine of the Trinity (1712). Clarke cited no less than
1,251 passages of Scripture to prove that God the Father was supreme,

and Christ and the Holy Spirit subordinate; this, he held, was the true Scriptural Trinity. Later Clarke edited the Book of Common Prayer to his liking, omitting the Athanasian Creed and other Trinitarian features.

As disbelief in the Athanasian doctrines grew more widespread in the Church of England, the question arose whether the Antitrinitarian clergy could continue sincerely to subscribe to the Church's doctrinal articles. Clarke encouraged what came to be called "Arian subscription"—assent in spite of doctrinal doubts. Arian subscription was the first step to non-subscription, and thus to outright Unitarianism.

Meanwhile the Dissenters (i.e., Protestants who had left the Church of England—mostly Presbyterians, Independents [Congregationalists], and Baptists) grew rapidly in strength. Their rights restored by the Toleration Act of 1689, they built chapels (the Church of England reserved the term "Church" for its own use), organized schools, and in other ways exercised their new freedom to worship as they pleased. But before long, as might have been expected, the Dissenters themselves began to part company over doctrinal differences. Increasing numbers of ministers became Unitarian in their thinking, some bringing their congregations with them, others being ejected from their pulpits. A local controversy spawned the first avowedly Antitrinitarian church in Exeter in 1719.

The so-called Salters' Hall conference, called later in 1719 to pacify the situation in Exeter and restore harmony among the Dissenters, resulted instead in permanent schism over the question of subscription. A majority at the conference, willing to subscribe to the traditional formulations of the Trinity, withdrew. The minority who remained became the nucleus of the liberal movement among the Dissenters. Their key principles were freedom of thought and congregational independence. Though heretical, they were, on the whole, well-educated, wealthy, and cultured, and their ministers, including Nathaniel Lardner and John Taylor of Norwich, were persons of outstanding ability.

The opposition to subscription within the Church of England had smoldered throughout the century. It reached a climax in 1771 in a petition, signed by more than two hundred Established clergy and laity, urging Parliament to abolish subscription. This would have allowed persons of liberal as well as orthodox persuasion to become ministers in the Church of England. Parliament overwhelmingly defeated the petition, largely on the basis of the argument that it would admit to the ministry heretics whose efforts would undermine the Established Church. Of the signers of the petition the vast majority accepted Parliament's decision and continued to subscribe. Five or six withdrew from the Church.

One of these, Theophilus Lindsey (1723-1808), was the organizer of the first Unitarian congregation in England. Using a reformed order of service based on Samuel Clarke's revision of sixty years earlier, and robed without the traditional white surplice, Lindsey conducted the first service in an auction room on Essex Street, London, on April 17, 1774. It was attended by a large congregation including Benjamin Franklin and Joseph Priestley. Here is Lindsey's account of the occasion, contained in a letter to a friend the next day.[13]

You will be pleased to hear that every thing passed very well yesterday; a larger and much more respectable audience than I could have expected, who behaved with great decency and in general appeared, and many of them expressed themselves, to be much satisfied with the whole of the service. Some disturbance was apprehended, and forboded to me by great names,—but not the least movement of the kind. The only fault found with it, was that it was too small. From the impressions that seemed to be made, and the general seriousness and satisfaction, I am persuaded that this attempt will, through the divine blessing, be of singular usefulness. The contrast between ours and the church-service strikes every one. Forgive me for saying, that I should have blushed to have appeared in a white garment. No one seemed in the least to want it. I am happy not to be hampered with any thing,—but entirely easy and satisfied with the whole of the service: a satisfaction never before known.—I must again say it, and bless God for it, that we were enabled to begin well. And we only desire to go on as through his blessing we have begun. . . .

The formation of the Essex Street congregation soon inspired other Unitarian "chapels" to be built in Birmingham, Manchester, and other English cities. Ecclesiastical independence fostered doctrinal freedom, so much so that in 1790, in an address to the students of

Oxford and Cambridge, Lindsey asserted the following "facts, clear
and plain to every understanding, . . . which all men, who believe
the scriptures, sooner or later must bow down to and acknowledge."[14]
With these almost modern convictions, English Unitarianism entered its greatest age.

(1) That there is ONE GOD, one single person, who is God, the
sole creator and sovereign lord of all things;

(2) That the holy JESUS was a man of the jewish nation, the
servant of this God, highly honoured and distinguished by him; and,

(3) That the SPIRIT, or HOLY SPIRIT, was not a person, or intelligent being; but only the extraordinary power or gift of God, im-
parted, first (Acts i. 2) to our Lord Jesus Christ himself, in his
life-time; and, afterwards, to the apostles, and many of the first
christians, to impower them to preach and propagate the gospel
with success: and

(4) That this was the doctrine concerning God, and Christ, and
the holy Spirit, which was taught by the apostles, and preached to
jews and heathens.

Alongside Lindsey emerged a second pioneer of English Unitarianism—Joseph Priestley (1733-1804). History remembers Priestley as
a scientist (he discovered oxygen in 1774), author, and cleric.
Priestley probably would have reversed the order, giving first priority
to his work as a minister. Wilbur pronounces him "beyond doubt
the most influential figure in the earlier history of the Unitarian
movement in England."

Educated at a Dissenting academy, Priestley found himself on the
heretical side of most theological questions. As a young minister
and teacher he studied the Scriptures only to find, like Servetus before him, that they provided meager support for the doctrines of
the Church, notably the Trinity and the atonement (i.e., the belief
that through the death and resurrection of Jesus Christ humankind's
sins are forgiven and divine justice is satisfied). He later described
his pilgrimage as a "passing from Trinitarianism to high Arianism,
from this to low Arianism, and from this to Socinianism."

Priestley's intellectual brilliance and broad interests attracted to
him some of the finest thinkers of his age including Benjamin
Franklin, Thomas Jefferson, and Richard Price.

His main contribution to English Unitarianism was a comprehensive argument, both historical and philosophical, for liberal Christianity—drawn from Scripture and early Christian writings, interpreted by reason, and rigorously applied to the religious and political problems of his day. "Absurdity supported by power," he wrote, "will never be able to stand its ground against the efforts of reason."

Of all of Priestley's religious works, probably the most influential was his History of the Corruptions of Christianity in two volumes, in which he sought to show that true Christianity, embodied in the beliefs of the primitive church, was Unitarian, and that all departures from that faith were corruptions. The Corruptions infuriated the orthodox and delighted the liberals in both England and America. It was publicly burned in Holland. Here follows Priestley's own summary.[15]

To consider the system (if it may be called a system) of christianity a priori, one would think it very little liable to corruption, or abuse. The great outline of it is, that the universal parent of mankind commissioned Jesus Christ, to invite men to the practice of virtue, by the assurance of his mercy to the penitent, and of his purpose to raise to immortal life and happiness all the virtuous and the good, but to inflict an adequate punishment on the wicked. In proof of this he wrought many miracles, and after a public execution he rose again from the dead. He also directed that proselytes to his religion should be admitted by baptism, and that his disciples should eat bread and drink wine in commemoration of his death.

Here is nothing that any person could imagine would lead to much subtle speculation, at least such as could excite animosity. The doctrine itself is so plain, that one would think the learned and the unlearned were upon a level with respect to it. And a person unacquainted with the state of things at the time of its promulgation would look in vain for any probable source of the monstrous corruptions and abuses which crept into the system afterwards. Our Lord, however, and his apostles, foretold that there would be a great departure from the truth, and that something would arise in the church altogether unlike the doctrine which they taught, and even subversive of it.

In reality, however, the causes of the succeeding corruptions did then exist; and accordingly, without anything more than their natural operation, all the abuses rose to their full height; and what is more wonderful still, by the operation of natural causes also, without any miraculous interposition of providence, we see the abuses gradually corrected, and christianity recovering its primitive beauty and glory.

The causes of corruptions were almost wholly contained in the established opinions of the heathen world, and especially the philosophical part of it; so that when those heathens embraced christianity they mixed their former tenets and prejudices with it. Also, both Jews and heathens were so much scandalized at the idea of being disciples of a man who had been crucified as a common malefactor, that christians in general were sufficiently disposed to adopt any opinion that would most effectually wipe away this reproach.

The opinion of the mental faculties of man belonging to a substance distinct from his body or brain, and of this invisible spiritual part, or soul, being capable of subsisting before and after its union to the body, which had taken the deepest root in all schools of philosophy, was wonderfully calculated to answer this purpose. For by this means christians were enabled to give to the soul of Christ what rank they pleased in the heavenly regions before his incarnation. On this principle went the Gnostics, deriving their doctrine from the received oriental philosophy. Afterwards the philosophizing christians went upon another principle, personifying the wisdom, or logos of God the Father. But this was mere Platonism, and therefore cannot be said to have been unnatural to their circumstances, though at length they came, in the natural progress of things, to believe that Christ was, in power and glory, equal to God the Father himself.

From the same opinion of a soul distinct from the body came the practice of praying, first for the dead, and then to them, with a long train of other absurd opinions, and superstitious practices.

The abuses of the positive institutions of christianity, monstrous as they were, naturally arose from the opinion of the purifying and sanctifying virtues of rites and ceremonies, which was the very basis of all the worship of the heathens; and they were also similar to the abuses of the Jewish religion. We likewise see the rudiments of all the monkish austerities in the opinions and practices of the heathens, who thought to purify and exalt the soul by macerating and mortifying the body.

As to the abuses of the government of the church, they are as easily accounted for as abuses in civil government; worldly minded men being always ready to lay hold of every opportunity of increasing their power; and in the dark ages too many circumstances concurred to give the christian clergy peculiar advantages over the laity in this respect.

Upon the whole, I flatter myself that, to an attentive reader of this work, it will appear, that the Corruption of Christianity, in every article of faith or practice, was the natural consequence of the circumstances in which it was promulgated; and also that its recovery from these corruptions is the natural consequence of different circumstances. . . .

To bring the whole [of opinions concerning Christ] into a short compass, the first general council gave the Son the same nature with the Father, the second admitted the Holy Spirit into the Trinity, the third consigned to Christ a human soul in conjunction with the eternal Logos, the fourth settled the hypostatical union of the divine and human nature of Christ, and the fifth affirmed, that in consequence of this union the two natures constituted only one person. It requires a pretty good memory to retain these distinctions, it being a business of words only, and ideas not concerned in it.

Under the leadership of Lindsey and Priestley, English Unitarianism after 1774 mushroomed in numbers, chapels, and confidence. As minister of the New Meeting chapel in Birmingham, Priestley preached Unitarianism, pamphleteered, and worked tirelessly for liberal and unpopular causes including the French Revolution, all the while carrying on his scientific experiments. On Bastille Day, July 14, 1791, a mob, aroused by Church of England leaders, destroyed Priestley's home, laboratory, and library, and ravaged all the Unitarian chapels in Birmingham. Priestley escaped to London. The following Sunday he sent a sermon to be read to his congregation on the text, "Father, forgive them; for they know not what they do." In 1794 he sailed for America to begin life anew and there, in Northumberland, Pennsylvania, to establish the first church in the United States to call itself Unitarian.

Priestley is often thought to be the founder of Unitarianism in America. He was not. American Unitarianism had its roots deep in colonial religion. Priestley enlarged and accelerated a religious move-

ment which had started one hundred and fifty years before among
the colonists themselves. We now turn to the development of liberal
religion in America.

Liberal Christianity in New England developed within Puritanism
as a threefold assertion: (1) of human goodness and free will against
the Calvinistic doctrine of original sin; (2) of the unity of God
against the prevailing doctrine of the Trinity; and (3) of the necessity of employing reason in interpreting Scripture. The decline in
the number of conversions—sudden religious experiences required
for full church membership—had the effect of loosening the Church's
grip on the people, and encouraging the rise of new bases of religious authority—reason and conscience. The early leaders of liberal
thought were solitary ministers who became convinced by their own
reading and conversation of the falsehood of the accepted doctrines.
Through their preaching many of the oldest and wealthiest families
in New England gave up Calvinism and slipped into liberalism without knowing it.

But the orthodox ministers knew it and were alarmed. Some of
them attempted to stem the tide of "infidelity" by encouraging a
spectacular religious revival beginning in 1734—the Great Awakening. Its leaders were Jonathan Edwards, a Congregational minister
in Northampton, Massachusetts, and George Whitefield, a British
Methodist preacher who travelled from town to town. The revival
called forth a strong reaction from the liberals. One of them,
Charles Chauncy (1704-1787), minister of the First Church in
Boston, catalogued its excesses in a book called Seasonable Thoughts
on the State of Religion in New-England.[16]

There is not a Man, in the Country, in the sober Exercise of his
Understanding, but will acknowledge, that the late religious Stir
has been attended with many Irregularities and Disorders. These,
some are pleased to call, Imprudencies, human Frailties, accidental
Effects only, such as might be expected, considering the Remains
of Corruption in good Men, even among those in whom a remarkable Work of Grace is carrying on: others are in the Opinion, they
make a main Part of the Appearance that has been so much talk'd
of, and have arisen unavoidably, in the natural Course of Things,
from the Means and Instruments of this Appearance; and that it
could not reasonably be suppos'd, it should have been other wise.

I shall particularly show what these bad and dangerous Things are; making such Remarks (as I go along) as may be thought needful to set Matters in a just and true Light.

Among the bad Things attending this Work, I shall first mention Itinerant Preaching. This had its Rise (at least in these Parts) from Mr. WHITEFIELD; though I could never see, I own, upon what Warrent, either from Scripture or Reason, he went about Preaching from one Province and Parish to another, where the Gospel was already preach'd, and by Persons as well qualified for the Work, as he can pretend to be. . . .

And what is the Language of this going into other Men's Parishes? Is it not obviously this? The settled Pastors [he says] are Men, not qualified for their Office, or not faithful in the Execution of it; They are either unfit to take the Care of Souls, or grossly negligent in doing their duty to them: or, the Language may be, we are Men of greater gifts, superior Holiness, more acceptableness to GOD; or have been in an extraordinary Manner sent by him. Some of these Itinerants, 'tis evident, have travelled about the Country preaching, under the full Persuasion of an immediate Call from GOD: And as to most of them, it may be feared, the grand Excitement, at the Bottom, has been, an overfond Opinion of themselves, and an unchristian one of their Brethren. It has, therefore been their Practice, too commonly, not only to boast of their own superior Goodness, wherever they have gone; but to insinuate suspicions against the fixed Pastors, if not to preach against them, and pray for them, as poor, carnal unconverted Men: Nay, meer Candidates for the Ministry. . . .

Moreover, what is the Tendency of this Practice, but Confusion and Disorder? If one Pastor may neglect his own People to take Care of others, who are already taken Care of . . . I say, if one Pastor may do this, why not another, and another still, and so, 'till there is no such Thing as Church Order in the Land? . . . And if this should become the general Practice, what might be expected, as the Effect, but an intire Dissolution of our Church State? This Itinerant Preaching, it is my firm Persuasion, naturally tends to it in the Course of Things; yea, and the Principles, upon which it is supported, will disband all the Churches in the World; and make the Relation, between Pastors and People, a meer Nothing, a Sound without Meaning. . . .

The next Thing I shall take Notice of, as what I can't but think of dangerous Tendency, is that Terror so many have been the Subjects of; Expressing itself in strange Effects upon the Body, such as swooning away and falling to the Ground, where Persons have lain, for a Time, speechless and motionless; bitter Shriekings and Screamings; Convulsion-like Tremblings and Agitations, Strugglings and Tumblings, which, in some Instances, have been attended with Indecencies I shan't mention; None of which Effects seem to have been accidental, nor yet peculiar to some particular Places or Constitutions; but have been common all over the Land. . . . It ought to be carefully remembered, the Passion of Fear may be excited, not only from a just Representation of Truth to the Mind by the SPIRIT of GOD, but from the natural Influence of awful Words and frightful Gestures. . . .

The next Thing to be considered, as what I can't but look upon to be of dangerous Tendency is that sudden Light and Joy so many, of late, claim to be the Subjects of. . . . But then, there is a false, as well as true Joy; the Joy of the Hypocrite, as well as of the real Christian. . . . Laughing, so far as I am acquainted with the History of the Church, is a Method of expressing religious Joy peculiar to the present Times: Nor can I think from whence it should take Rise, unless from Mr. WHITEFIELD and TENNENT. The former of these Gentlemen was sometimes observed to speak of the affairs of Salvation, with a Smile on his Countenance; but 'tis generally known of the latter, that he could scarce hear of a Person's being under the slightest Conviction, but he would laugh. . . . [This practice] seems inconsistent with that holy Fear and Caution, which must be thought reasonable, where the Salvation of the Soul is the Thing it is conversant about. . . .

The next Thing that is amiss, and very much so, in these Times, is that Spirit of rash, Censorious, and uncharitable Judging [against the Ministers] which has been so prevalent in the Land. This appear'd, first of all, in Mr. w——D [Whitefield], who . . . had an evident Tendency to fill the Minds of People with evil Surmisings against the Ministers, as tho' they were, for the most Part, carnal, unregenerate Wretches. . . . [Yet] May it not be said of the Body of the Ministers, in New-England, that they are a Set of Men, as sound in the Faith, and of as good a Life, as any Part of the Christian World are favored with?

Chauncy's attack on the errors of the Great Awakening was the opening wedge between liberal and conservative Congregationalists. Thereafter the liberals grew bolder, and the two wings of the Church began imperceptibly to split apart.

In 1749 Jonathan Mayhew (1720-1766), the young minister of the West Church in Boston, preached and published Seven Sermons, the most lucid and advanced statement of Arminian liberalism of its day. Instead of the Calvinist God of judgment and punishment, Mayhew described a "wise and infinitely gracious being" who seeks the happiness of all his creatures. To this end God gives us reason, and it is by reason that "we resemble God himself." Mayhew further argued that we are endowed with the capacity to distinguish right and wrong and to choose the right (the central doctrine of Arminianism). The trustworthiness of reason and conscience led Mayhew to champion the right of private judgment in religion, a right which was to become the key principle not only of American Unitarianism but of American democracy itself.[17]

1st Let us all stand fast in the liberty wherewith Christ has made us free; and not suffer ourselves to be intangled with any yoke of bondage. If we have submitted to the yoke hitherto, and ingloriously subjected ourselves to any human impositions in religious matters; it is better to throw off the yoke even now, than to let it gall us all our life-time: It is not yet too late to assert our liberty, and free ourselves from an ignominious slavery to the dictates of men.

Let us take pains to find out the truth, and after we are settled in our judgment concerning any religious tenet or practice, adhere to it with constancy of mind, till convinced of our error in a rational way. Let us despise the frowns and censures of those vain conceited men who set themselves up for the oracles of truth and the standard of orthodoxy; and then call their neighbors hard names—We have not only a right to think for ourselves in matters of religion, but to act for ourselves also. Nor has any man whatever, whether of a civil or sacred Character, any authority to control us, unless it be by the gentle methods of argument and persuasion. To Christ alone, the supreme and only head of the christian church, and the final judge of mankind; to him alone we are accountable for not believing his doctrines, and obeying his commandments, as such. And whosoever attempts to restrain or control us, takes it upon him to rule another man's servant, forgetting that he also is a man under authority; and must hereafter stand or fall by a sentence from the same mouth with ourselves.

Did I say, we have a right to judge and act for ourselves? I now add—it is our indispensible duty to do it. This is a right which we cannot relinquish, or neglect to exercise, if we would, without being highly culpable; for it is absolutely inalienable in its own nature. We may dispose of our temporal substance if we please; but God and nature and the gospel of Christ injoin it upon us to maintain the right of private judgment, and to worship God according to our consciences, as much as they injoin us to give alms to the poor, to love God and our neighbor, and practice universal righteousness: and we may as well talk of giving up our rights to the latter, as to the former. They are all duties, and not rights simply; duties equally founded in the reason of things; duties equally commanded by the same God; duties equally required in the same gospel. . . .

But

2ly. And to conclude, while we are asserting our own liberty and Christian rights, let us be consistent and uniform; and not attempt to incroach upon the rights of others. They have the same right to judge for themselves and to choose their own religion, with ourselves. And nothing is more incongruous than for an advocate of liberty, to tyrannize over his neighbors. We have all liberty to think and act for ourselves in things of a religious concern; and we ought to be content with that, without desiring a liberty to oppress and grieve others. . . . Let us, as much as in us lies, live peaceably with all men; but suffer none to lord it over our consciences. . . . Let us use no methods but those of sober argument and kind persuasion, in order to bring men over to a belief and practice of the truth as it is in Jesus. . . .

From Chauncy and Mayhew's view of the benevolence of the deity, the logical next step was the belief that God in his goodness would assure the salvation of all persons, not just an elected few as the Calvinists held. Indeed, in the 1760's Chauncy wrote a full-length book arguing from Scripture that all sinners must ultimately be reconciled to God.

The doctrine that God would draw all humanity to himself at the

Last Judgment is almost as old as Christianity itself. Origen of
Alexandria (185-254), an early Christian writer, was a universalist.
His doctrine was declared heretical in 553 A.D. More recently, in
1552, Universalism was outlawed in King Edward VI's forty-two
articles of religious conformity, the last of which read, "They also
deserve to be condemned who endeavor to restore that pernicious
opinion that all men (though never so ungodly) shall at last be
saved; when for a certain time, appointed by the Divine Justice,
they endured punishment for their sins committed." In 1562 the
forty-two articles were reduced to thirty-nine, with this one omitted.
Since then Universalism has been legal in England and its adherents,
though few in number, have been forceful and outspoken. Universalist sentiment in the American colonies centered in New England and eastern Pennsylvania.

In 1770 an English Universalist, John Murray (1741-1815), arrived
by ship in Good Luck, New Jersey, hoping to retire from the trage-
dies of his former life and die peacefully in America. A disciple of
the London Universalist preacher James Relly, and an intimate of
the Methodist leaders Wesley and Whitefield, Murray was, in spite
of his wishes, immediately pressed into service as a preacher, first in
New Jersey, later as a travelling preacher. He was welcomed by those
who sought relief from the awful prospect of eternal damnation,
and opposed by the settled ministers, including Chauncy, and by
heresy-hunting laity. After several years of itinerant preaching he
wrote Relly as follows.[18]

The severity with which I am reproached, has hitherto been pro-
portioned to my success; and I am of course, in this town, the object of inveterate hatred. But I am about to commence a long
journey, to visit many towns where I have many, or what is better,
where my divine Master hath many friends. . . .

My first stage after quitting B[oston], will be the town of
P[rovidence]; from thence to N[ew] P[ort], where I have preached
much, and where my labour hath not been in vain in the Lord. A
religious character undertook to write against me, and thus helped
the cause he aimed to destroy. In N[ew] P[ort] there are some faithful souls. I shall next proceed to N[orwich], in Connecticut, where
there are a great number who attend with delight, upon a preached

gospel, and who are neither forgetful nor unprofitable hearers of the word. From N[orwich], I pass to N[ew] L[ondon]. I have not associated with any disciples of our Lord who are more sincere than those believers who have their residence in this city; they walk in the light, are invigorated by the beams of the sun of righteousness, and greatly refreshed by those doctrines which distil as the dew, as the small rain, upon the tender herb, and as the showers upon the grass.

My next preaching stage is G[uilford], where, although I always preached as I pass and repass, there are but few who acknowledge the force of divine truth. From G[uilford] I shall go on to F[air-field?]; I have frequently almost resolved to preach no more in F[airfield]; I never laboured in this place with any visible success; and although there be many in this town who flock to hear me, yet as I do not believe they understand what they hear, I am inclined to think I am not sent there [by God]. From thence I proceed to N[ew] R[ochelle?], the first stage in New-York government. In N[ew] R[ochelle] there are some who know the truth, and the truth hath made them free: the hearts of those believers rejoice whenever I make my appearance among them, for they contemplate fresh discoveries of the Redeemer's grace: there are beside these, in N[ew] R[ochelle], many who seem attached to me, but I declare I scarcely know for what; and although gratified whenever I am the object of attention, let the motive producing such attention be ever so remote or obscure, yet I am abundantly better pleased to receive but a cup of cold water from a disciple, in the name of a disciple. Real disciples must undoubtedly be friends of the Saviour; and such, I am persuaded will be abundantly more to the praise and glory of divine grace, and more steadfast in their friendship to the humble instrument of their information.

The radical "good news" that Murray preached caused him to be sought out by all kinds of persons. Once a minister, on hearing him, clasped him in his arms exclaiming, "If this be heresy, may I so worship the God of my fathers, during the residue of my days." Another time a deacon approached him skeptically. Murray gives this account of their conversation.[19]

DEACON. I have heard much of you, and have come many miles to see and converse with you. Will you be so obliging as to permit me to ask a few questions?

MURRAY. Readily, Sir.

DEACON. I have heard—but I do not pay much regard to slanderous reports; nothing of that sort is to be depended upon— But I have heard— Excuse me, Sir, I really hope you will not be angry, but indeed, Sir, I have heard, I have been told, that you preached Universal Salvation, that is, that all mankind will be saved.

MURRAY. Well, Sir, as you seem to be an honest man, I will freely own to you, that God hath told me, "That he sent not his Son into the world, to condemn the world, but that the world through him might be saved."

DEACON. Aye, the *believing* world.

MURRAY. No, Sir; the world are never called believers, nor believers the world. The Deacon then proceeded to mention a variety of scriptures, that proved, as the poor man believed, the damnation of the greatest part of the world, and I answered him from the same scriptures: At last, I mention that very obnoxious text, "As in Adam all die, so in Christ shall all be made alive."

DEACON. Aye, Sir, all that believe.

MURRAY. No, Sir, all who died in Adam.

DEACON. But, how can they be made alive in Christ without believing?

MURRAY. As well as they could die in Adam without believing. There are a very great multitude among mankind, who do not believe they died in Adam; and as they do not believe they died in Adam, then they did not die in Adam.

DEACON. O yes, Sir, they died in Adam, whether they believe it or not.

MURRAY. How can they, Sir, die in Adam without believing they did?

DEACON. Because the word of God declares, "they died in Adam," and that must be true whether they believe it or not.

MURRAY. But, Sir, the same word of God says, all shall be made alive in Christ; and yet you say it is only those who believe, that shall be made alive!

This silenced the old gentleman, and thus ended our conversation;

but another and another succeeded, until half past two o'clock, when I proceeded to a more public delivery of my testimony. . . .

Murray was a moderate Calvinist (he retained the doctrine of election, but universalized it) and a Trinitarian. He proved universal salvation from the Bible, choosing to speak in the language of Scripture because "it expresses my own ideas better than any set of phrases I could press into my service."

Of all the Scripture prooftexts employed by Murray, the most significant appear to have been: "For as in Adam all die, even so in Christ shall all be made alive" (I Cor. 15:22); "God was in Christ, reconciling the world unto himself" (II Cor. 5:19); and "Behold the Lamb of God, which taketh away the sin of the world" (John 1:29). The last was the text of one of Murray's great sermons, from which a paragraph is quoted below. We do not know where it was preached—perhaps in Gloucester, Massachusetts, where he was minister of the Independent Church of Christ from 1780 to 1793, or in Boston at the First Universal Church where he served until his death in 1815.[20]

Jesus, therefore, is either a complete Saviour, or he is no Saviour at all. He, by the grace of God, tasted death for every man, or he tasted death for no man. He bore all our sins in his own body on the tree, or he bore none at all. He put all our sins away by the sacrifice of himself, or none at all. He was the propitiation for the sins of the whole world, or for no individual in the world. God was in Christ reconciling the world unto himself, or he reconciled no one to himself. Jesus is made sin for all, or for none. He has made peace for all, or for no one child of Adam. His righteousness is upon all, or upon no one; he is all in all, or of little consequence to any one.

While Murray was preaching universal salvation, the full tide of liberal opinion in eastern Massachusetts was Antitrinitarian. Mayhew, influenced by correspondence with English Dissenters, in 1755 published a book openly ridiculing the Athanasian doctrine of the Trinity. An orthodox minister lamented, "Men of figure are bold enough to deride and banter the sacred doctrines of Christianity, and despise our orthodox confessions of faith." The next year Emlyn's Humble Inquiry was anonymously reprinted in Boston.

Although the main thrust of Antitrinitarian sentiment lay in the Congregational churches, the first church to avow Unitarian beliefs was not Congregational but Episcopal—the First Episcopal Church in Boston (King's Chapel), founded in 1686. Its pulpit vacant, the Wardens in 1782 invited James Freeman (1759-1835), a young Congregational graduate of Harvard, to be lay reader until an Episcopal candidate could be found. Freeman accepted, but soon found the Trinitarian creeds and prayers in the Book of Common Prayer incompatible with his Socinian views. When he explained his conflict to the congregation it supported him and voted to change the liturgy. Freeman and a committee of the congregation made the revisions and published the new liturgy with the following preface.[21]

Many truly great and learned men, of the Church of England, as well divines as laymen, have earnestly wished to see their Liturgy reformed; but hitherto all attempts to reform it have proved ineffectual. The late happy revolution here hath forever separated all the Episcopal Societies, in the United States of America, from the Church of England, of which the King of that country is the supreme head, and to whom all ArchBishops, Bishops, Priests, and Deacons of that Church are obliged to take an oath of allegiance and supremacy, at the time of their consecration or ordination. Being torn from that King or Church, the Society for whose use this Liturgy is published, think themselves at liberty, and well justified even by the declarations of the Church of England, in making such alterations, as "exigency of the times and occasions hath rendered expedient," and in expunging everything which gave, or might be suspected to give, offense to tender consciences; guiding themselves however by "the holy scriptures, which," they heartily agree with the Church of England, "contain all things necessary to salvation," and that "whatsoever is not read therein, nor can be proved thereby, is not to be required of any man, that it should be believed as an article of faith, or be thought requisite or necessary to salvation." In the 34th of the Articles of the Church of England, it is declared, That "it is not necessary that traditions and ceremonies be in all places one, or utterly like; for at all times they have been diverse, and may be changed according to the diversity of countries, times, and men's manners, so that nothing be ordained against God's word." And by the 20th of those Articles it is declared, that "the Church hath power to decree rites and ceremonies, and authority in controversies of faith." What is there meant by the word Church will appear from the 19th of those Articles, which declares "The visible Church of Christ is a Congregation of faithful men, in which the pure word of God is preached, and the sacraments be duly ministered, according to Christ's ordinance, in all those things that of necessity are requisite to the same. As the Church of Jerusalem, Alexandria, and Antioch have erred, so also the Church of Rome hath erred, not only in living, and manner of ceremonies, but also in matters of faith." At the Reformation, when the Book of Common Prayer of the Church of England was compiled, the Committee appointed to execute that business were obliged to proceed very tenderly and with great delicacy, for fear of offending the whole body of the people, just torn from the idolatrous Church of Rome; and many things were then retained which have, in later times, given great offence to many, truly pious Christians.

The Liturgy, contained in this volume, is such, that no Christian, it is supposed, can take offence at, or find his conscience wounded in repeating. The Trinitarian, the Unitarian, the Calvinist, the Arminian will read nothing in it which can give him any reasonable umbrage. God is the sole object of worship in these prayers; and as no man can come to God, but by the one Mediator Jesus Christ, every petition is here offered in his name, in obedience to his positive command. The Gloria Patri, made and introduced into the Liturgy of the Church of Rome by the decree of Pope Damasus, towards the latter part of the fourth century, and adopted into the Book of Common Prayer, is not in this Liturgy. Instead of that doxology, doxologies from the pure word of God are introduced. It is not our wish to make proselytes to any particular system or opinions of any particular sect of Christians. Our earnest desire is to live in brotherly love and peace with all men, and especially with those who call themselves the disciples of Jesus Christ.

In compiling this Liturgy great assistance hath been derived from the judicious corrections of the Reverend Mr. Lindsey, who hath reformed the Book of Common Prayer according to the Plan of the truly pious and justly celebrated Doctor Samuel Clarke. Several of Mr. Lindsey's amendments are adopted entire. The alterations which are taken from him, and the others which are made, excepting the prayers for Congress and the General Court, are none of them novelties; for they have been proposed and justified by some of the first divines of the Church of England.

On the premise of the strict unity of God all prayers to the Trinity were omitted or modified. The Nicene Creed was omitted and the Apostle's Creed edited to exclude the clauses "He descended into hell" and "The Holy Catholic Church." Special services such as the communion and baptism were shortened and modernized. The Unitarian doxology incorporated in place of the traditional Gloria Patri (i.e., "Glory be to the Father") appeared as below.[22] To ascribe glory to God through Jesus Christ was permissible; but to ascribe glory to Jesus and the Holy Ghost—never.

The liturgy reform was followed in 1787 by another extraordinary event—the ordination of Freeman by the King's Chapel congregation when no bishop would agree to ordain him. Thus did Freeman serve King's Chapel until his death in 1835—the first Unitarian minister of the first Unitarian church in the United States.

BOOK OF COMMON PRAYER	KING'S CHAPEL REVISION
Min. O Lord, open thou our lips;	Min. O Lord, open thou our lips;
Ans. And our mouth shall show forth thy praise.	Ans. And our mouth shall show forth thy praise.
Min. O God make speed to save us;	Min. O God make speed to save us;
Ans. O Lord make haste to help us;	Ans. O Lord make haste to help us;
Min. Glory be to the Father, and to the Son, and to the Holy Ghost;	Min. Now unto the King eternal, immortal, invisible, the only wise God;
Ans. As it was in the beginning, is now, and ever shall be, world without end. Amen.	Ans. Be honour and glory, through Jesus Christ for ever and ever. Amen.
Min. Praise ye the Lord.	Min. Praise ye the Lord.
Ans. The Lord's name be praised.	Ans. The Lord's name be praised.

Independence was the overmastering goal of the American colonists during the 1770's and 1780's. The King's Chapel reforms were impulses of the same movement that produced the Battles of Lexington and Concord, the Battle of Bunker Hill, indeed, the Revolutionary War itself.

The most explicit advocate of the American independence movement was not a New Englander but a Virginian—Thomas Jefferson (1743-1826). Although born of aristocratic parents and baptized into the Church of England, Jefferson's political and religious ideas were decidedly liberal. He trained for a career in law and politics. When he arrived at the Second Continental Congress in Philadelphia in 1775, he already possessed, as John Adams remarked, "a reputation for literature, science, and a happy talent of composition." Jefferson's authorship of the Declaration of Independence in 1776 at the age of thirty-three placed him in the front ranks of the revolutionary leaders.

In 1779 Jefferson composed another "declaration of independence," this one designed to free the people of Virginia from spiritual tyranny. By the time of the revolution a majority of the inhabitants had become dissenters from the Church of England. Yet every voting citizen was required to pay taxes to support the Church. To correct this injustice Jefferson prepared a historic resolution granting to all Virginians complete freedom of religious belief, and abolishing compulsory taxation for a church to which the majority of people were no longer loyal. The resolution was adopted in 1786 as the "Statute of Virginia for religious freedom." [23] Its principles of religious equality and the separation of church and state were later written into the basic law of the United States as the First Amendment to the Constitution.

Well aware that Almighty God hath created the mind free; that all attempts to influence it by temporal punishments or burdens, or by civil incapacitations, tend only to beget habits of hypocrisy and meanness, and are a departure from the plan of the Holy Author of our religion, who being Lord both of body and mind, yet chose not to propagate it by coercions on either, as was in his Almighty power to do; that the impious presumption of legislators and rulers, civil as well as ecclesiastical, who, being themselves but fallible and uninspired men have assumed dominion over the faith of others, setting up their own opinions and modes of thinking as the only true and infallible, and as such endeavoring to impose them on others, hath established and maintained false religions over the greatest part of the world, and through all time; that to compel a man to furnish contributions of money for the propagation of opinions which he disbelieves, is sinful and tyrannical; that even the forcing him to support this or that teacher of his own religious persuasion, is depriving him of the comfortable liberty of giving his contributions to the particular pastor whose morals he would make his pattern, and whose powers he feels most persuasive to righteousness, and is withdrawing from the ministry those temporal rewards, which proceeding from an approbation of their personal conduct, are an additional incitement to earnest and unremitting labors for the instruction of mankind; that our civil rights have no dependence on our religious opinions, more than our opinions in physics or geometry; that, therefore, the proscribing any citizen as unworthy the public confidence by laying upon him an incapacity of being called to the offices of trust and emolument, unless he profess or renounce this or that religious opinion, is depriving him injuriously of those privileges and advantages to which in common with his fellow citizens he has a natural right; that it tends also to corrupt the principles of that very religion it is meant to encourage, by bribing, with a monopoly of worldly honors and emoluments, those who will externally profess and conform to it; that though indeed these are criminal who do not withstand such temptation, yet neither are those innocent who lay the bait in their way; that to suffer the civil magistrate to intrude his powers into the field of opinion and to restrain the profession or propagation of principles, on the supposition of their ill tendency, is a dangerous fallacy, which at once destroys all religious liberty, because he being of course judge of that tendency, will make his opinions the rule of judgment, and approve or condemn the sentiments of others only as they shall square with or differ from his own; that it is time enough for the rightful purposes of civil government, for its offices to interfere when principles break out into overt acts against peace and good order; and finally, that truth is great and will prevail if left to herself, that she is the proper and sufficient antagonist to error, and has nothing to fear from the conflict, unless by human interposition disarmed of her natural weapons, free argument and debate, errors ceasing to be dangerous when it is permitted freely to contradict them.

Be it therefore enacted by the General Assembly, That no man shall be compelled to frequent or support any religious worship, place or ministry whatsoever, nor shall be enforced, restrained, molested, or burthened in his body or goods, nor shall otherwise suffer on account of his religious opinions or belief; but that all men shall be free to profess, and by argument to maintain, their opinions in matters of religion, and that the same shall in nowise diminish, enlarge, or affect their civil capacities.

And though we well know this Assembly, elected by the people for the ordinary purposes of legislation only, have no power to restrain the acts of succeeding assemblies, constituted with the powers equal to our own, and that therefore to declare this act irrevocable, would be of no effect in law, yet we are free to declare, and do declare, that the rights hereby asserted are the natural rights of mankind, and that if any act shall be hereafter passed to repeal the present or to narrow its operation, such an act will be an infringement of natural right.

In his thinking about the universe, Jefferson was a deist. The deists believed that God created the universe and invented laws to operate it—the laws of nature. We perceive and understand these laws by means of our capacity to reason.

In this kind of universe a supernatural "savior," such as the Church believed Christ to be, was impossible or, if possible, unnecessary. To the deists Jesus was important only as a teacher and exemplar of the good life. The virtuous individual was one who fostered human rights—life, liberty, and the pursuit of happiness. The only God was "Nature's God."

Jefferson and Benjamin Franklin were the most famous American deists. They became the intellectual leaders of the American enlightenment which a generation later blended with New England liberalism to produce the Unitarian movement.

Jefferson's deistic views of religion are nowhere more clearly presented than in a letter he wrote to his nephew, Peter Carr, in 1787.[24]

Your reason is now mature enough to examine this object [religion]. In the first place, divest yourself of all bias in favor of novelty and singularity of opinion. Indulge them in any other subject rather than that of religion. It is too important, and the consequences of error may be too serious. On the other hand, shake off all the fears and servile prejudices, under which weak minds are servilely crouched. Fix reason firmly in her seat, and call to her tribunal every fact, every opinion. Question with boldness even the existence of a God; because, if there be one, he must more approve of the homage of reason, than that of blindfolded fear. You will naturally examine first, the religion of your own country. Read the Bible, then, as you would read Livy or Tacitus. The facts which are within the ordinary course of nature, you will believe on the authority of the writer, as you do those of the same kind in Livy and Tacitus. The testimony of the writer weighs in their favor, in one scale, and their not being against the laws of nature, does not weigh against them. But those facts in the Bible which contradict the laws of nature, must be examined with more care, and under a variety of faces. Here you must recur to the pretensions of the writer to inspiration from God. Examine upon what evidence his pretensions are founded, and whether that evidence is so strong, as that its falsehood would be more improbable than a change in the laws of nature, in the case he relates. For example, in the book of Joshua, we are told, the sun stood still several hours. Were we to read that fact in Livy or Tacitus, we should class it with their showers of blood, speaking of statues, beasts, etc. But it is said, that the writer of that book was inspired. Examine, therefore, candidly, what evidence there is of his having been inspired. The pretension is entitled to your inquiry, because millions believe it. On the other hand, you are astronomer enough to know how contrary it is to the law of nature that a body revolving on its axis, as the earth does, should have stopped, should not, by that sudden stoppage, have prostrated animals, trees, buildings, and should after a certain time have resumed its revolution, and that without a second general prostration. Is this arrest of the earth's motion, or the evidence which affirms it, most within the law of probabilities? You will next read the New Testament. It is the history of a personage called Jesus. Keep in your eye the opposite pretensions: 1, of those who say he was begotten by God, born of a virgin, suspended and reversed the laws of nature at will, and ascended bodily into heaven; and 2, of those who say he was a man of illegitimate birth, of a benevolent heart, enthusiastic mind, who set out with pretensions to divinity, ended in believing them, and was punished capitally for sedition, by being gibbeted, according to the Roman law, which punished the first commission of that offence by whipping, and the second by exile, or death *in furea*. . . .

Do not be frightened from this inquiry by any fear of its consequences. If it ends in a belief that there is no God, you will find incitements to virtue in the comfort and pleasantness you feel in its exercise, and the love of others which it will procure you. If you find reason to believe there is a God, a consciousness that you are acting under his eye, and that he approves you, will be a vast additional incitement; if that there be a future state, the hope of a happy existence in that increases the appetite to deserve it; if that Jesus was also a God, you will be comforted by a belief of his aid and love. In fine, I repeat, you must lay aside all prejudice on both sides, and neither believe nor reject anything, because any other persons, or description of persons, have rejected or believed it. Your own reason is the only oracle given you by heaven, and you are answerable, not for the rightness, but uprightness of the decision. . . .

Unitarianism broke its chains during the nineteenth century. The chain of doctrine, which bound previous generations to the Bible and to Christ, was cast off leaving all persons free to seek and affirm God within themselves as Reason, Soul, and Conscience. The chain of class, whose links were Wealth, Title, and Learning, was sundered by English missionaries like Richard Wright, who believed that simple people could understand a simple religion better than anybody else, and by American preachers like Theodore Parker, who recognized only two classes of people—the free and the unfree—and sought to make humankind one. The chain of fear, forged by centuries of bigotry and oppression, fell when the people discovered their leaders—Martineau, Channing, Parker—and the leaders discovered their God. Thus freed from the shackles of tradition and circumstance, Unitarianism embraced Unitarian Christianity, Transcendentalism, and Naturalism in such rapid succession that the radicalism of Boston in 1819 was the conservatism of Cambridge in 1838 and the anachronism of Chicago in 1880. Unitarianism also became the mind and pen of America as the Nation sought to discover where it was, where it had been, and where it was going. It was a magnificent century, one, like those of Jesus and Luther, to be relived and ploughed back into the future.

The successor of Priestley and Lindsey in the leadership of the English churches was Thomas Belsham (1750-1829), who, like Biddle a century before him, had been converted to Unitarianism while teaching orthodoxy to the young. In rapid succession Belsham became minister at the Gravel Pit church in Hackney (where Priestley had served between the Birmingham riots and his departure for America) and at Lindsey's Essex Street Chapel in London. Under Belsham's leadership the scattered Unitarian churches coalesced into a distinct movement, with the formation of new congregations in northern England, Wales, and Ireland, the establishment of societies to distribute books and tracts, and the adoption of a strictly human view of Jesus, discarding Arianism.

The main cause of Unitarian growth was missionary preaching among the working people. The first missionaries were settled ministers who preached in nearby towns. One such was Richard Wright (1764-1836), who became the "perpetual missionary" sponsored by the Unitarian Fund for Promoting Unitarianism by Popular Preaching. Wright often walked forty miles a day to organize scores of new Unitarian churches between 1792 and 1822. Here is his account of a missionary experience in Yorkshire.[25]

In the early part of the summer of 1805, while with my friend Mr. [William] Vidler in London, he received a letter from a person at Thorne in Yorkshire; in which letter the writer said, that some persons in that town and its neighborhood, who were inclined to the doctrine of the universal restoration, were anxious to hear and converse with a preacher who maintained that doctrine; that they had heard of a preacher of that description who sometimes traveled in Lincolnshire; but knew not his address; that if he would visit them they would be glad to hear him, and would willingly entertain him. Mr. Vidler handed the letter to me as the person to whom the writer referred, and advised me to visit Thorne. A few weeks after, I conducted my eldest daughter to Hull, where she had engaged to go as an assistant teacher in a boarding school: and from Hull went on to Thorne which is forty miles from that town. As I approached Thorne on the Saturday in the afternoon, my feelings were much excited, and my mind considerably exercised. I was entering on a new scene of action, where I was a total stranger; I knew nothing of the people but what the letter before mentioned had communicated, and that did not give the names of any of them. For the writer of the letter only could I inquire, and he might be dead since the time of writing it; and what his character was, I knew not. I felt the importance of the mission in which I was now engaged, my heart was raised to God, I prepared myself for action in the best manner I could, and derived strength from on high. With such feelings I entered Thorne, and walked through a considerable part of the town, pondering the course I should take. At length, seeing a barber's shop I turned in to get shaved, but my chief object was to gain information respecting the character of the

person for whom I had to inquire. I found he was in humble circumstances, but to my satisfaction learned he was a man of good
character; of course I made the best of my way to his house. I had
written at least, a week before hand, to inform him of my intended
visit. On my arrival at his house I found he was not within; but his
wife said, you are the gentleman we were expecting. I walked in
and made myself quite free, which I have ever found to be the best
way, especially with persons in humble circumstances. The good
man soon came in, and I found they had engaged a lodging for me
at the house of a widow woman who was a methodist; to which I
soon after retired. In a short time a pretty large company came
about me, and we arranged matters respecting the Sunday. It was
determined that I should preach three times, in a barn, which had
been engaged for the purpose, and public notice was given accordingly. I found the people were Methodists, chiefly of the new connection [i.e., orthodox]. They had either given up the doctrine of
endless punishment, or doubted the truth of it; but retained the
other doctrines of reputed orthodoxy.

We soon got into conversation on religious subjects, and Dr.
Priestley's name happened to be mentioned, I perceived it excited
alarm, which led me to ask if any of them had known him or seen
any of his writings. They replied they had neither known him nor
seen any of his writings; but had learned that he was a very bad
man, and maintained very dangerous doctrines. I said of his doctrines, I will now say nothing, but I will give you some account of
his character. This I accordingly did, in particular of the manner
in which he had borne ill treatment and persecution, and the spirit
which he had manifested towards his persecutors; and warned them
against giving implicit credit to what they heard about men and
their doctrines of whom they had no personal knowledge. This I
perceived had a good effect. After we had talked some time, my
hostess said, "I hope, sir, you are not an Arian." I replied, "No, I
am not, I never was an Arian." She rejoined, "Had you been an
Arian, I dared not have let you sleep in my house." Had she known
as much of me as she did some time after, she would have thought
me still worse than an Arian; but at the time she had no idea of any
thing more frightful than an Arian: nor did I find lodging at her
house after my first visit.

On the Sunday almost the whole town, and many people from

the neighboring villages, came together to hear me; the barn was crowded, and many stood on the outside; all seemed deeply attentive. They had heard of me as an Universalist preacher, and knew nothing further of me. I expected that so soon as they understood my views, as an Unitarian, their prejudices would be alarmed, and the multitude would be dispersed; but I thought there were a few individuals among them who would adhere to me, and that ultimately a congregation would be established: and thus it turned out. On the Sunday morning I preached on the love of God, in the afternoon, on the doctrine of reconciliation, and in the evening, on future punishment. After the evening service we had a large party together for conversation; and before we parted I told them, both in public and in private, as I thought they were then capable of bearing, that, if I lived to see them again, I should have many more things to communicate to them: and I entreated them not to be afraid of thinking freely on all subjects, not to think any thing too sacred to be examined, not to deem any doctrine false, merely because it was generally thought to be false, nor to conclude any doctrine to be true merely because it was generally received as truth; but to bring every thing to the test of reason and scripture, and to be determined to judge for themselves. We parted in the most friendly manner, and they urged me to visit them again. . . .

In the following winter I revisited Thorne, and found that after my former visit a great alarm had been created respecting my sentiments as a Unitarian; the alarm had risen to such a height, that some persons had thought of writing to me not to go there any more; but this had been prevented by others. A person had been from Thorne to the north marshes of Lincolnshire, and brought back with him my work called the "Antisatisfactionist," a number of letters which I had written to persons in those marshes, on a variety of religious subjects. For these the people at Thorne were not yet prepared. However, I found, that by reading of them, notwithstanding the alarm excited, several persons had become Unitarians. During my second visit I preached many times at a granary, and had good congregations, though not such a multitude as I had at the first. I had much conversation with different persons, and brought them into a plan of meeting together to worship the one God, read the scriptures and such other books as might improve and edify them, and to do what they could for the establishment and promotion of the cause. Thus Unitarianism was now planted at Thorne, in the midst of a district where it was before unknown. . . .

During the second quarter of the nineteenth century the English Unitarians, while worshipping freely, were forced to defend their property against the claims of the orthodox Dissenters. The most damaging blow came in the Lady Hewley Charities case of 1842 which prohibited the Unitarians the use of monies and property which, having been established under orthodox auspices, had through the course of time devolved into Unitarian hands. The rule of law applied in this case was that a trust could not be held for any purpose that would have been illegal at the time it was made. As a result the Unitarians were not only deprived of substantial income but were also faced with the prospect of losing—through court action —all of their historic chapels. To prevent this, Parliament was persuaded to rule in the Dissenters' Chapels Act that long undisputed possession of property creates a vested right. The Unitarian chapels were thus secured to Unitarian use, and a new era of expansion begun.

The most influential English Unitarian of the nineteenth century was James Martineau (1805-1900), the tall, gaunt teacher and theologian of Manchester New College. Martineau displaced the miracle-based Scriptural theology of Lindsey and Priestley with new affirmations based on reason and intuition. In his emphasis on the soul as the source of spiritual experience, Martineau became philosophically a kin of the American Transcendentalists. His hymns are sung throughout the Unitarian world.

Martineau's view of Unitarian history, his transcendental idealism, and his luminous use of the English language are revealed in the following address given in 1869, entitled "Three Stages of Unitarian Theology." [26]

The strength of the Unitarian faith lies in the very first position which it seized, and which I hold to be the impregnable centre of all true religious and moral theory,—that, for all spiritual natures, Unity and Personality are One. That which distinguishes you from another, and holds you to your identity from day to day, is the permanent Self-consciousness which the stream of varying thoughts touches as it flows, and the continuous Will which issues or permits the most opposite activities. These are the highest and characteristic attributes of our being; and by its highest attributes must every nature be measured, and in them must its essence be found. Suppose them to change: let a fever obliterate your memory of the past, or establish within you a double and alternate consciousness, unrelated as your dreaming to your day; and we could no more call to account this fluctuating Self than we could punish John for Peter's lie. The moral identity once broken, all other continuity goes for nothing; all other sameness is illusory. What boots it that you are still as tall, as strong, as swift as you were before; that your friends recognize your photograph and your voice; that your pulse has not altered its speed, nor your brain its size? your being has fallen into fragments which these threads are ineffectual to blend. This rule of thought is our only guide when we pass to things Divine; and it compels us to say that, if God be not One Person, he is not One at all: whatever else remains, when you have multiplied the Personal centres of thought and will, is lower than these, and any Unity it may have is of no interest to us; for whom nothing Impersonal can ever be Divine. The Godhead, if by that you mean the Supreme Object of our worship and our trust, subsists not in any spiritual substance within whose compass separate Personalities may have their presence and unfold their celestial drama; but in the living seats of Infinite Mind and perfect holiness: a plurality of these is a plurality of Gods; and if you try to integrate them again by a common relation to some impersonal essence, you do but deify the lower after taking away the unity from the higher.

. . . The first essential then of a restored purity of worship was precisely the work to which our predecessors in the last century addressed themselves:—to clear the Personality of God, till it is simple as the unity of the soul: to sweep away the haze of ancient Pantheism, with the ecclesiastical mythology it holds: to take the eternal Son of God from heaven, and isolate the Father, as the One Infinite Mind, the Sole Self-subsisting Life, the all-pervading Will, at whose disposal creation lies.

The first effect of this absolute loneliness of God inevitably was to exhibit the universe as a stupendous centralized monarchy, administered on one plan, and directed by one power. The provinces of the Cosmos can thus have, as it were, no municipal life; the local agents no real independence: the whole hierarchy of place and rank is but the receptacle and organ of a force given and transmitted: there can be no pause for remonstrance, no idea of resistance. . . .

In vindicating the Sovereignty of the universal Father, this scheme subordinates the whole universe alike, and allows nothing to approach nearer to him than the web to him that weaves it: the threads may be of this colour or of that, in the warp or in the woof; but all are interwoven in the same texture, and hold a homogeneous relation to the Maker. Man, therefore, is not less exclusively a part of nature, than the birds and the plants; is worked up in the same way into the organism of the world; and though he may have a larger consciousness, containing within itself more successive links in the chain of production, is equally the theatre of their predetermined order, and powerless to give them an alternative direction. He too, like all else, is as the clay to the potter, to be moulded by another; and be the pressure on the inside or on the out, he is shaped and does not shape himself. . . .

The reaction [to this view of God's relation to man] naturally came from the other end of the relation between us and God. As, in the *Religion of Causation*, Man seemed to be crushed into a mere creature, so was it on his behalf that remonstrance broke forth, and, at the bidding of Channing, the *Religion of Conscience* sprang to its feet. However fascinating the precision and simplicity of the Necessarian theory in its advance through the fields of physical and biological law, it meets with vehement resistance in its attempt to annex human nature, and put it under the same code with the tides and trees and reptiles. Our personality, though frightened and dwindled for a moment and hardly believing its own voice, is sure to recover from the most ingenious philosophy, and to re-assert its power over the alternatives before it, and own its obligation to the authority within it; and the second period of our theology is marked by this recovered sense of Moral Freedom. When the tones of the New-England prophet reached us here, why did they so stir our hearts? They brought a new language; they burst into a forgotten chamber of the soul; they recalled natural faiths which had been explained away, and boldly appealed to feelings which had been struck down; they touched the springs of a sleeping enthusiasm, and carried us forward from the outer temple of devout science to the inner shrine of self-denying Duty. The very inspiration of the new Gospel, in what thought does it lie? The greatness of human capacity, not so much for intellectual training, as for voluntary righteousness, for victory over temptation, for resemblance to God. . . . If you gaze down upon the human race from the Causal throne of the universe, they [humanity's heroes and saints] are flung into insignificance and float as gleaming dust upon the air-current. But if from the interior of the human spirit you look up to the heaven of God, you find a possible divineness in man, and an affinity with the Original perfection, which dissipates the illusion of his littleness. . . .

If now we put together the two types of doctrine which I have described, and make them into one, so far as they are compatible, shall we find rest in a complete and adequate theology? . . . No. . . . There is in us that which is above the natural life, and apprehends what lies beyond it; and just as God is not imprisoned in the universe, but transcends it, and in that outlying realm is hindered by no pledge from acting freely out of fresh affections, so have we a range of free ideal life, whence we can look down upon the instincts of nature and up to the infinite Holiness, and which we know is in subjection to nothing inflexible. This is precisely what we mean by Spirit,—this liberty to move alternatively out of the thought and love of a reasonable mind; God is a Spirit, in so far as he is not locked up in the invariable order of the world: and there is a spirit in Man, in so far as he is not disposed of by his organism and his dwelling-place, but rises in thought and directs himself in affection to what is above them. Here then it is that there is room for true communion,—that Spirit may meet Spirit, and that the sacred silence may itself speak the exchange of love. Our moral ideals, the irrepressible sigh after higher perfection, the sense of Divine authority in every vision of the better, the shame at every yielding to the worse, these, we are well aware, are not of our making, or donations of other men; they are above us; they are given to us; they are what draw us to God, and commence our likeness to him. In this field of spiritual affection that lies around our will, the common essence of man and God, the divine element that spreads its margin into us, has its home, its life, its reciprocal recognition; its bursts of human prayer, its answer of Divine compassion; its deep shadows of contrition, and returning gleams of restoration. The life with God then, of which saintly men in every age have testified, is no illusion of enthusiasm, but an ascent, through simple surrender, to the higher region of the soul, the very watchtower whence there is the clearest and largest view. The bridge is thus complete between the Divine and the human personality; and we crown the religion of Causation, and the religion of Conscience, by the religion of the Spirit. . . .

Since 1900—the year of Martineau's death—the English Unitarians, like all England's Protestants, have struggled to maintain their strength and vitality in the face of two World Wars, a deteriorating economy, and a steady decline in denominational morale. Many persons—among them Philip Henry Wicksteed, the Dante scholar and sociologist of religion; Alexander Gordon, the Unitarian historian; L. P. Jacks, the teacher and essayist; and E. G. Lee, the editor of The Inquirer—have given outstanding intellectual leadership. But in spite of all efforts the movement has declined: between 1900 and 1938 average total attendance at Sunday services dropped from approximately 42,000 to 13,500; and in 1942 more than one-third of the Unitarian churches in England had no church schools. The denomination has been burdened with antiquated administrative machinery, and ministerial recruitment has lagged—the teaching profession and the Armed Forces claiming many otherwise qualified persons. Finally—a fact which cannot but startle American Unitarians—46 of the 334 Unitarian churches in Britain were damaged or destroyed by enemy action during World War Two, and the denomination's headquarters at Essex Hall, London, totally destroyed. Economic conditions have made rebuilding expensive and in many cases impossible.

In spite of these sobering trends, however, in the years since the war English Unitarianism has shown signs of new vigor with able, imaginative individuals entering its ministry, intensified contacts between the English and American churches, and a sense of realistic determination evident in such affirmations as this from "The Work of the Churches" (1946): "Altogether, then, we have considerable resources; 24,000 people with a mission and a purpose, backed by financial aid, are in a great position to conduct a long-term mission on behalf of their faith. Instead of thinking of themselves as the remnants of a defeated army they should regard themselves as a determined body of people ready to go forward in the work which is essentially dear to each one of them. The present is not a time for looking backward but for seizing the immense opportunities presented by the future."

Meanwhile in eastern Massachusetts at the turn of the nineteenth century, Unitarianism had slowly and silently prevailed. The shift to liberalism, though it involved a large majority of the churches east of Worcester including eight of nine in Boston, was regarded as only a "vague unrest." The old Congregational order was still unbroken.

The break between the liberal and orthodox Congregationalists came dramatically in 1805 when a liberal, Henry Ware (1764-1845), was elected Professor of Divinity at Harvard College. Harvard was the oldest college in the United States, the fountainhead of New England culture, and the stronghold of liberal Congregationalism. The Hollis Professorship of Divinity, established in 1721 by Thomas Hollis, a London merchant, was the oldest endowed professorship in America.

This post had fallen vacant in 1803 at the death of Professor David Tappan. Liberal majorities in the Harvard Corporation (a six-person administrative council presided over by the President) and Board of Overseers (a body of sixty-five religious and governmental leaders including the ministers of six nearby churches, holding veto power over faculty appointments) sought Ware's immediate election. The conservative minority, led by the Rev. Jedidiah Morse of Charlestown, stalled for time, hoping to elect a suitably orthodox person. At length, on February 1, 1805, the Corporation chose Ware. He was confirmed by the Overseers on February 14 by a vote of 33 to 23.

Soon afterward, Morse published a pamphlet explaining his stand, "The True Reasons on which the Election of a Hollis Professor . . . was opposed." [27] To prove the orthodoxy of Harvard College and of Thomas Hollis, Morse quoted the motto of the College seal —"Christo et Ecclesiae," For Christ and the Church—and the clause in Hollis' orders specifying a person "of sound or orthodox principles." (The liberals had circumvented this clause by pointing out that the only article of belief Hollis had required of the Divinity Professor at his inauguration should be "that the Scriptures of the Old and New Testament are the only perfect rule of faith and manners.")

Morse's pamphlet then continued,

Such, as have now been stated, are facts relative to the foundation of this Professorship, and such the qualifications and principles required by Mr. Hollis in his Professor, and sought and found by former electors. Things being so, when called upon at the Board of Overseers to concur with the Corporation in their choice of a Hollis Professor of Divinity, it was conceived proper and necessary to inquire, Does the candidate possess the qualifications required by the founder? Is he of sound or orthodox principles? Did the electors, previous to their choice, examine the candidate, as was done in the case of the first two Professors, as to his orthodoxy? These questions were accordingly asked, but no satisfactory answers were given. It was observed that the candidate had not been examined by the Corporation, and the propriety of such a procedure was doubted. The right to examine, indeed, was denied. The particular religious principles of the candidate, though often asked for, were not disclosed, and are, it is believed, still unknown to a great part of the members of the Board, except so far as they may be inferred from the silence of his friends, from negative evidence, and from his catechism. It was particularly asked by one of the honorable members of the Senate, whether the candidate was a believer in that important doctrine, the divinity of the Lord Jesus Christ? The reply conveyed no precise or satisfactory answer on that point. While thus ignorant of the "principles" of the candidate, how could the board determine whether or not they were "sound or orthodox" whatever be the meaning of these terms? From the catechism published by the Candidate, it was inferred, that he was not a Calvinist; that his sentiments on important points, such as the depravity of human nature, the impotency of man, the character of Jesus Christ, and the future state of the wicked, were widely different from those of Dr. Watts, whose catechism he professedly followed as his "model," in compiling his own, so closely, indeed, as in general to adopt the same questions and answers.†

---

† The following specimen will show the reader the difference between Dr. Watts' and Mr. Weare's [Ware's] Catechism, on some important and distinguishing doctrinal points.

DR. WATT'S CATECHISM, 2D PART

33. Q. Whence comes it to pass that you have been such a sinner?

A. I was born into this world with inclinations to that which is evil; and I have too much indulged these inclinations all my life.

MR. WEARE'S CATECHISM, 2D PART

Q. 43. Whence came it to pass that you have been such a sinner?

A. I became so by an unguarded and foolish indulgence of my irregular appetites and passions, in opposition to the law written in my heart, and to the plain dictates of the holy Scriptures.

We have seen the singular anxiety and caution of Mr. Hollis by his letters, and by a bond to secure the object of his Foundation, and to guard his professorship against error and innovation in all future time. Now if barriers so sacred can be removed, what guard can be devised, which shall secure any bequest against violation? What assurance can any well disposed persons in future have, that any donations, they may wish to make to Harvard College, will be applied to their objects, even one century? How this will effect

---

34. Q. How came you to be born with such an inclination to evil?

A. All men are born in sin, because they come from Adam, the first man who sinned against God.

Omitted

41. Q. Is not Jesus Christ God as well as man?

A. Though he be a man, yet he is God also; for he is a glorious person in whom God and man are joined together and his name is Immanuel, or God with us.

Omitted

43. Q. How could Christ obtain pardon and life for us by his doing or suffering?

A. Our sins had deserved death, but Christ was the Son of God, and perfectly righteous, and God appointed him to suffer death, to take away our sins, and to bring us into his favour.

Part 3d. Q. 4. How could Christ obtain pardon and life for us, by his doing and suffering?

A. By the gracious appointment of the Father, who was pleased to accept the obedience of Christ unto death, as a vindication of his righteous government in granting pardon to penitent sinners, and raising them to a happy immortality.

50. Q. Is not your heart itself sinful, and have you power of yourself to repent of sin, and to truth in Christ, and obey him?

A. We have sinful hearts, and cannot do these duties ourselves; but God has promised his own holy spirit, if we pray for it, to renew our hearts to holiness, and help us to do his will.

Omitted

54. Q. What is Baptism?

A. It is a washing with Water in the name of the Father, the Son, and the Holy Spirit.

Q. 17. What is Baptism?

A. It is a solemn washing with water, as a sign, or distinguished mark of our belonging to the visible church of Christ, who has enjoined a compliance with this rite, upon all who believe his gospel, and hope for Salvation through him.

There appears to be nothing in Mr. Weare's catechism which an Arminian, Arian, or a Universalist on Dr. Chauncy's scheme would not readily subscribe.

this change in the religious character of the Professorship, and of the University will gradually and ultimately produce in the state of our Churches, and on the religious and moral character of our citizens, cannot with so much certainty be foreseen. In respect to New England, it is an untried experiment. GOD forbid, that this change should be injurious and ruinous; that in consequence, the faith of our churches should become less pure, their discipline less strict, the difference lessened between those, who professedly serve God, and those who avowedly serve him not; till at length the spirit and power of our religion shall have evaporated, and its very forms be abolished.

"For CHRIST and the CHURCH," was this ancient college founded by men, whom we delight to call our Fathers; "for CHRIST and the CHURCH" has it hitherto been cherished, instructed and governed by men of like christian principles and spirit; "for CHRIST and the CHURCH" Oh may the GOD of our Fathers, who still lives and reigns, in mercy preserve it, so long as the sun and the moon shall endure!

Ware's election as Divinity Professor shattered the unity of Massachusetts Congregationalism. In spite of the unsectarian intentions of the liberals, Jedidiah Morse viewed their rise as a conspiracy to undermine orthodoxy. Harvard having "fallen" to the Unitarians, Morse and his sympathizers in 1808 established the Andover Theological Seminary to train persons in the orthodox tradition. In Conrad Wright's words, "The Arminian movement had done its work; the Unitarian Controversy had begun."

In the same year (1805) a young Universalist minister serving churches in rural Vermont, Hosea Ballou (1771-1852), published a Treatise on Atonement which argued the liberal position in theology with great cogency.[28] Ballou's treatise also inaugurated a new era in theological method by proving its case not only from Scripture but by the force of simple logic. For its fresh language and reasoning the Treatise makes exciting reading even today.

It is recorded that once after Ballou had preached in John Murray's Boston pulpit, a worshiper in the front pew rose and said to the congregation, "I wish to give notice that the doctrine that has been preached here this afternoon is not the doctrine which is usually preached in this house." So it was. Singlehandedly Ballou moved Universalist thinking from a Calvinistic to a Unitarian base by asserting that God was Father rather than Judge, that Jesus was an exalted human being rather than a person of the Trinity, and that sin was personal rather than inherited. In Ballou, Universalism caught the reason and hope of the times and became a vision of salvation for thousands of Americans, including William Ellery Channing himself.

The plan of redemption, as held by many, may be reduced to the following compendium. God, from all eternity, forseeing that man would sin, provided a Mediator for a certain part of his posterity, who should suffer the penalty of the law for them, and that these elect ones, chosen by God for the rest of mankind, will alone be benefitted by the atonement; that, in order that the sacrifice might be adequate to the crime, for which, the sinner was condemned to everlasting or endless suffering, God himself, assumed a body of flesh and blood, such as the delinquent was constituted in, and suffered the penalty of the law by death, and arose from the dead. By this process, the demand of the law was completely answered, and the debt due to Divine Justice, by the elect, was fully and amply paid. But that this atonement does not affect those who were not elected as objects of mercy, but that they are left to suffer endlessly for what Adam did, before they were born. It is true, they are a little cautious about saying that God himself absolutely died! But they say, that Christ, who was crucified, was really God himself, which must, in effect, amount to the same thing. And in fact, if the Infinite did not suffer death, the whole plan falls, for it is by an infinite sacrifice that they pretend to satisfy an infinite dissatisfaction.

Why the above ideas should ever have been imbibed, by men of understanding and study, I can but scarcely satisfy myself; their absurdities are so glaring, that it seems next to impossible, that men of sobriety and sound judgment should ever imbibe them, or avoid seeing them.

As reason will not consent to the plan of God, as described in the foregoing scheme, I will show that the scriptures equally oppose it. It is granted, that Jesus Christ died for mankind, as the scriptures declare; but not in the way, in which thousands have believed. But supposing he died instead of the sinner, in the way which I dispute, I still wish to prove, that he died for the whole of Adam's posterity, as much as he did for any. [Ballou then quotes Isaiah 53:5-6, I Tim. 2:5-6, I John 2:1-2, and Hebrews 2:9.] The above scriptures, with the connexions and corresponding passages, as fully prove that Christ died for ALL men, as any one thing can be proved from the bible. Now, as there is not, in all the scripture, a single hint to the reverse of these passages which I have introduced, it appears strange and unaccountable to me, that any person, who professes to believe the testimony of the bible, should ever have entertained the idea, that what these passages say, is false, and that which is not said, in contradiction to what is, is true! . . .

I close this work, humbly hoping and expecting the glorious increase and extensive growth of what I have, (though feebly) contended for, viz. the holiness and happiness of mankind. I look, with strong expectation, for that period, when all sin, and every degree of unreconciliation will be destroyed, by the divine power of that love which is stronger than death, which many waters cannot quench, nor the floods drown; in which alone I put my trust, and in which my hope is anchored for all mankind; earnestly praying, that the desire of the righteous may not be cut off.

The fulness of times will come, and the times of the restitution of all things will be accomplished. Then shall truth be victorious, and all error flee to eternal night. Then shall universal songs of honor be sung to the praise of him who liveth forever and ever. All death, sorrow and crying, shall be done away; pains and disorders shall be no more felt, temptations no more trouble the lovers of God, nor sin poison the human heart. The blessed hand of the once crucified shall wipe tears from off all faces. O, transporting thought! Then shall the blessed Savior see of the travail of his soul, and be satisfied, when, through his mediation, universal nature shall be brought in perfect union with truth and holiness, and the spirit of God fill all rational beings. Then shall the law of the spirit of life in Christ Jesus, which maketh free from the law of sin, become the governing principle of the whole man once made subject to vanity, once inthraled in darkness, sin and misery; but then, delivered from the bondage of corruption, and restored to perfect reconciliation to God, in the heavenly Adam. Then shall the great object of the Savior's mission be accomplished. Then shall the question be asked, O death, where is thy sting? But death shall not be, to give the answer. And, O grave, where is thy victory? But the boaster shall be silent. The son shall deliver up the kingdom to God the Father; the eternal radiance shall smile, and GOD shall be ALL in ALL.

In the decade after 1805 the Unitarians steadily gained strength. The Jeffersonian revolution was confirming the individualism and enlarging the tolerance of New Englanders. Channing and Joseph Stevens Buckminster preached liberal Christianity to growing numbers of Bostonians, great and small. Unitarian journals brought articles, reviews, and sermons to a large audience of readers. As ideologies formed, communication between liberals and the orthodox diminished, and tension increased. By 1815 Massachusetts Congregationalism was a house divided in everything but name.

The Unitarians did not like the Unitarian name. Morse had called Henry Ware a Unitarian in 1805, but the label was rejected by Ware's friends as a "calumny." To them it signified partisanship and controversy, theological narrowness and sectarian exclusiveness. They preferred the title "liberal Christian."

In 1815 Morse rudely and cleverly forced the Unitarian name on the liberals against their wishes. He accomplished this by distributing under the title "American Unitarianism," a chapter from Thomas Belsham's Memoir of Theophilus Lindsey published three years earlier in London. Here are excerpts from "American Unitarianism." [29]

The grand theological controversies which excited so much attention, and were conducted with so much animosity, in England, could not fail to attract notice in America, and especially in the New-England States, where a manliness of character, a decency of morals, and a serious though not universally enlightened spirit of piety, dispose the minds of considerable numbers to religious enquiries, and where freedom of investigation suffers no restraint from the civil power. It was with great pleasure that Mr. Lindsey received information in the year 1786 . . . that the principal Episcopalian Church in Boston had consented to the introduction of a Liturgy reformed nearly upon the plan of that which had been adopted in Essex-Street and perfectly Unitarian.

As a further means of diffusing the important doctrines of the proper Unity of God, and the simple humanity of Jesus Christ, Mr.

Lindsey made a present of his own and of Dr. Priestley's Theological Works to the Library of Harvard College, in the University of Cambridge in New-England; for which, "as a very valuable and acceptable present," he received the thanks of the President and Fellows. These books were read with great avidity by the students. But though there is great reason to believe that the seed thus sown took deep root, and that in many instances it produced an abundant harvest; and though many persons eminent for rank and talent in the New-England States openly avowed the Unitarian creed, it does not appear that any numerous societies of Christians have hitherto followed the example of the congregation at the King's Chapel in making a public profession of the Unitarian doctrine.

In March, 1792, an Unitarian congregation was formed at Portland, a considerable town of the district of Maine. . . . About the same time another society for Unitarian worship was formed at Saco, a populous village about twenty miles distant from Portland, under the auspices of Mr. Thatcher, a gentleman of large property and of excellent character, who was repeatedly returned as representative in Congress. . . . Another Unitarian congregation has been formed at Oldenbarneveld, a new settlement in the back country of the state of New-York. . . .

In the state of Massachusetts, and particularly in the environs of Boston, the great cause of Christian truth is making a silent but rapid and irresistible progress. From the inquisitive and liberal spirit which prevails in the University of Cambridge [i.e., Harvard], which has never been checked at any time, but which there is reason to expect will receive every requisite aid and encouragement from the present learned and accomplished Principal, Dr. Kirkland, the happiest consequences may be expected to ensue. . . .

The Monthly Anthology, the General Repository, and other valuable periodical publications, conducted by gentlemen of distinguished talents and liberality, tend very much to diffuse a spirit of inquiry. Bigotry is discountenanced; and, if I am not greatly misinformed, divine worship in many of the principal churches at Boston, is carried on upon principles strictly, if not avowedly Unitarian. Being myself a friend to ingenuousness and candour, I could wish to see all who are truly Unitarians openly such, and to teach the doctrine of the simple indivisible Unity of God, as well as to practice the rites of Unitarian worship. But I would not presume to judge for another. There may possibly be reasons for caution which do not occur to me, and of which I am not competent to judge. The time must however come, perhaps it is near, when truth will no longer endure confinement, but will burst forth in all her glory. The dull hollow rumbling at the bottom of the sea, which is scarcely noticed by the inattentive traveller who is gliding carelessly over the solid plate of ice which encrusts the surface, is, to the wary and experienced observer, a sure presage of the speedy and sudden explosion of the immense superincumbent mass, and of the restoration of the imprisoned waves to their native freedom, to the consternation and often to the utter distruction of those who refuse to listen to the friendly premonition.

Before the Unitarians could publicly clarify their differences with the English Unitarians, Morse published a "review" of "American Unitarianism" in his orthodox periodical, The Panoplist.[30] The purpose of the "review," which was written by Morse's friend Jeremiah Evarts, was to reinforce the glue on the Unitarian label as applied to the liberals. Specifically the review sought to show (1) that the liberals were Unitarians and therefore heretics; (2) that they had conspired in secret to overthrow the true faith; and (3) that they should be exposed and expelled from the Church. In actuality the Unitarian policy of co-operation, which the orthodox chose to interpret as sabotage, stemmed from a desire to maintain the solidarity of Christian faith and worship. But Morse's attack made this impossible, and separation inevitable.

We regard the appearance of this pamphlet as one of the most important events, which have taken place for many years, in reference to the interests of religion in our country. It has been known, for at least a quarter of a century, by those who have been well-informed on the subject, that there has been in Boston a defection from those doctrines of the Bible, which have usually been denominated orthodox in Protestant communities. It has been known, that this defection has gradually increased; has silently and covertly extended itself into a considerable number of congregations in the vicinity; and has been, in a few instances, openly avowed. From a great variety of anonymous publications it has been evident, that the defection had proceeded in the downward course to the lowest degrees of Socinianism, and to the very borders of open infidelity. Further than this;—it has not been in a few solitary instances only, that persons, who have been near the centre of all these operations, have heard from the pulpit both sermons and prayers, which neither expressed nor implied any thing more than sober Deism, and which were totally at variance with the Gospel. These things, and many more of a similar character, have warrented such disclosures through the medium of our work, and of other publications, as have fully apprized the Christian public of the existence of such a defection, as has been briefly described above. But as the work of error was carried on for the most part in secret;—as many well-meaning people were led in the dark;—and as proselytes were made principally by suppressing truth, rather than by explicitly proposing and defending error, it was a difficult matter so to expose the evil, as to present its character, extent, and design, in full view, before the eyes of its friends and its enemies. It has been an artifice practiced systematically by a majority of the clergymen, who have led the way in this apostasy from the faith of the Protestant churches, and, as we believe we may safely add, in this apostasy from Christianity, to inculcate the opinion, that they did not differ materially from their clerical brethren through the country. This artifice has been carried so far as to induce them to complain, in bitter terms, that they were slandered by our work, when represented as thus differing, and as promoting the circulation of Socinian books; although every representation, which we have made on the subject, has been warrented by most abundant evidence. They have complained, that they were not invited to preach when travelling through the country, and have imputed this neglect to the effect of slander. It is to be remembered, that the slander complained of is the allegation, that they differ essentially in religious doctrine from the great body of the American clergy. . . .

We should not be thus particular, were it not that the cry of calumny has been raised with considerable effect, and with the most unblushing confidence. But this cry cannot be raised here-after on the same account, and in the same manner. The pamphlet before us furnishes most decisive evidence, on the subject of the state of religion in Boston and vicinity. . . .

The writer [Belsham] has not gathered his information from a hasty survey of the exterior of the temple, which he describes; he has had access, as high priest of his order, to the very interior recesses, and has exposed to view the most secret transactions of those, who are initiated into the worship which he approves. He has shewn us, that like the Grecian philosophers of old, many of his order, in our country, would have one religion for the vulgar, and another for the wise; that it is a fundamental maxim among the great body of leading Unitarians here, not to expose their sentiments directly to the inspection of the world at large, and to challenge investigation, but to operate in secret; to entrust only the initiated with their measures; and to leave the vulgar to fall into the tracks of the wise, by the force of that principle of imitation which is capable of operating so powerfully upon them.

Our own convictions respecting the nature of Unitarianism in Massachusetts, and the manner in which the cause is promoted, are not altered by the pamphlet before us. Living in the centre of action, we have long had these convictions. The Monthly Anthology; the mangled Christian Monitor; . . . the Improved Version of the New Testament; all published in Boston; and especially the General Repository, published at Cambridge, by some of the officers of Harvard College, afford sufficient evidence, without detailing other circumstances, of a settled and persevering determination to prostrate orthodoxy, and to substitute Unitarianism in its place. . . .

The leader of Boston Unitarianism was William Ellery Channing (1780-1842). He stands as the colossus of American religious liberalism, with one foot planted in New England theology, the other in European rationalism, his vision raised high above that of his contemporaries, his soul nourished by the love of God, his voice beckoning the people to a more perfect freedom. In Channing's life and thought lies the best refutation of Morse's charge that Unitarianism was maliciously sectarian.

Channing was born and raised in Newport, Rhode Island, the son of a prominent lawyer and grandson of William Ellery, a signer of the Declaration of Independence. While his Calvinistic conditioning made him humble, his father's example and his Harvard education made him inquisitive. He was of small stature, self-disciplined, popular in spite of his intellectuality, and a natural leader.

Channing's religious thinking evolved from early belief in divine election to a belief that God bestowed his love on all persons, and from a belief in human depravity—including his own—to a conviction that we have an innate moral sense by which we perceive and can choose the good. His reading of the New Testament led him to see the unlimited potential of human goodness, but he was a grown man before he arrived at the basic affirmation of his theology, namely, that God's perfection is identical with our own, that through humane living all persons are, like Jesus, made one with God.

Channing was called to Boston's Federal Street Church in 1803. His ministry there lasted until his death in 1842, spanning the entire emergent period of American Unitarianism. Preaching was, in the phrase of one of his disciples, "the great action" of Channing's life. Channing regarded it as but a means to an end, namely "to act upon other minds, and to act through sympathy as well as instruction."

It was Channing, the prophet, preacher, and hero of New England Unitarianism, who in 1819 began a new epoch by proclaiming its faith fearlessly and unmistakably to the world. The occasion was the ordination of Jared Sparks in the new Unitarian church in Baltimore. The leading Unitarian ministers were there, including Henry Ware. Even before the sermon was given arrangements had been made to print 2,000 copies.

Channing entitled his sermon "Unitarian Christianity." The first part showed how Unitarians interpreted the Scriptures, the second outlined the Unitarian beliefs in God, the Trinity, Jesus, and Christian virtue.

The "Baltimore sermon" gave the Unitarians a platform and an advocate. It placed them for the first time on the offensive in relation to the orthodox. It was very probably the most important Unitarian sermon ever preached anywhere.[31]

Text: Prove all things; hold fast that which is good.—I Thessalonians v. 21

. . . I have thought it my duty to lay before you, as clearly as I can, some of the distinguishing opinions of that class of Christians in our country who are known to sympathize with this religious society. . . .

There are two natural divisions under which my thoughts will be arranged. I shall endeavor to unfold, 1st, The principles which we adopt in interpreting the Scriptures. . . .

(I) We regard the Scriptures as the records of God's successive revelations to mankind, and particularly of the last and most perfect revelation of his will by Jesus Christ. Whatever doctrines seem to us to be clearly taught in the Scriptures, we receive without reserve or exception. We do not, however, attach, equal importance to all the books in this collection. Our religion, we believe, lies chiefly in the New Testament. The dispensation of Moses, compared with that of Jesus, we consider as adapted to the childhood of the human race, a preparation for a nobler system, and chiefly useful now as serving to confirm and illustrate the Christian Scriptures. Jesus is the only master of Christians, and whatever he taught, either during his personal ministry, or by his inspired apostles, we regard as of Divine authority, and profess to make the rule of our lives. . . .

Our leading principle in interpreting Scripture is this, that the Bible is a book written for men, in the language of men, and that its meaning is to be sought in the same manner as that of other books. We believe that God, when he speaks to the human race, conforms, if we may so say, to the established rules of speaking and writing. . . .

. . . With these views of the Bible, we feel it our bounden duty to exercise our reason upon it perpetually; to compare, to infer, to look beyond the letter to the spirit, to seek in the nature of the subject, and the aim of the writer, his true meaning; and, in general, to make use of what is known for explaining what is difficult, and for discovering new truths. . . .

. . . In other words, we believe that God never contradicts, in one part of Scripture, what he teaches in another; and never contradicts, in revelation, what he teaches in his works and providence. . . .

We do not announce these principles as original or peculiar to ourselves. All Christians occasionally adopt them, not excepting those who most vehemently decry them when they happen to menace some favorite article of their creed. All Christians are compelled to use them in their controversies with infidels. All sects employ them in their warfare with one another. All willingly avail themselves of reason, when it can be pressed into the service of their own party, and only complain of it when its weapons wound themselves. . . .

We object strongly to the contemptuous manner in which human reason is often spoken of by our adversaries, because it leads, we believe, to universal skepticism. If reason be so dreadfully darkened by the fall, that its most decisive judgments on religion are unworthy of trust, then Christianity, and even natural theology, must be abandoned; for the existence and veracity of God, and the Divine original of Christianity, are conclusions of reason, and must stand or fall with it. . . .

We indeed grant, that the use of reason in religion is accompanied with danger. But we ask any honest man to look on the history of the Church, and say, whether the renunciation of it is not still more dangerous. . . .

(II) Having thus stated the principles according to which we interpret Scripture, I now proceed to the second great head of this discourse, which is, to state some of the views which we derive from that sacred book, particularly those which distinguish us from other Christians.

(1) In the first place, we believe in the doctrine of God's UNITY, or that there is one God, and one only. To this truth we give infinite importance, and we feel ourselves bound to take heed, lest any man spoil us of it by vain philosophy. The proposition, that there is one God, seems to us exceedingly plain. We understand by it, that there is one being, one mind, one person, one intelligent agent, and one only, to whom underived and infinite perfection and dominion belong. We conceive, that these words could have conveyed no other meaning to the simple and uncultivated people who were set apart to be the depositaries of this great truth, and who were utterly incapable of understanding those hairbredth distinctions between being and person which the sagacity of latter ages has discovered. We find no intimation, that this language was to be taken in an unusual sense, or that God's unity was a quite different thing from the oneness of other intelligent beings.

We object to the doctrine of the Trinity, that, whilst acknowledging in words, it subverts in effect, the unity of God. According to this doctrine, there are three infinite and equal persons possessing supreme divinity, called the Father, Son, and Holy Ghost. Each of these persons, as described by theologians, has his own particular consciousness, will, and perceptions. They love each other, converse with each other, and delight in each other's society. They perform different parts in man's redemption, each having his appropriate office, and neither doing the work of the other. . . . When we attempt to conceive of three Gods, we can do nothing more than represent to ourselves three agents, distinguished from each other by similar marks and peculiarities to those which separate the persons of the Trinity; and when common Christians hear these persons spoken of as conversing with each other, loving each other, and performing different acts, how can they help regarding them as different beings, different minds?

We do, then, with all earnestness, though without reproaching our brethren, protest against the irrational and unscriptural doctrine of the Trinity. . . . "God sent his Son." "God anointed Jesus." Now, how singular and inexplicable is this phraseology, which fills the New Testament, if this title belong equally to Jesus, and if a principal object of this book is to reveal him as God, as partaking equally with the Father in supreme divinity! We challenge our opponents to adduce one passage in the New Testament where the word God means three persons. . . . Can stronger proof be given that the doctrine of three persons in the Godhead is not a fundamental doctrine of Christianity?

. . . In the second place . . . we believe in the unity of Jesus Christ. We believe that Jesus is one mind, one soul, one being, as truly as we are, and equally distinct from the one God. We complain of the doctrine of the Trinity, that, not satisfied with making God three beings, it makes Jesus Christ two beings, and thus introduces infinite confusion into our conceptions of his character. This corruption of Christianity, alike repugnant to common sense and to the general strain of Scripture, is a remarkable proof of the power of a false philosophy in disfiguring the simple truth of Jesus. . . .

. . . I now proceed to another point on which we lay still greater stress. We believe in the moral perfection of God. We consider no part of theology so important as that which treats of God's moral character; and we value our views of Christianity chiefly as they assert his amiable and venerable attributes.

. . . We conceive that Christians have generally leaned towards a very injurious view of the Supreme Being. They have too often felt as if he were raised, by his greatness and sovereignty, above the principles of morality, above those eternal laws of equity and rectitude to which all other beings are subjected.

We believe, that in no being is the sense of right so strong, so omnipotent, as in God. We believe that his almighty power is entirely submitted to his perceptions of rectitude; and this is the ground of our piety. It is not because he is our Creator merely, but because he created us for good and holy purposes; it is not because his will is irresistible, but because his will is the perfection of virtue, that we pay him allegiance. We cannot bow before a being, however great and powerful, who governs tyranically. We respect nothing but excellence, whether on earth or in heaven. We venerate, not the loftiness of God's throne, but the equity and goodness in which it is established. We believe that God is infinitely good, kind, benevolent, in the proper sense of these words; good in disposition, as well as in act; good, not to a few, but to all; good to every individual, as well as to the general system. . . .

Having thus spoken of the unity of God; of the unity of Jesus, and his inferiority to God; and of the perfections of the Divine character; I now proceed to give our views of the mediation of Christ and of the purposes of his mission. With regard to the great object which Jesus came to accomplish, there seems to be no possibility of mistake. We believe that he was sent by the Father to effect a moral or spiritual deliverance of mankind; that is, to rescue men from sin and its consequences, and to bring them to a state of everlasting purity and happiness. We believe, too, that he accomplishes this sublime purpose by a variety of methods; by his instructions respecting God's unity, parental character, and moral government, which are admirably fitted to reclaim the world from idolatry and impiety to the knowledge, love, and obedience of the Creator, by his promises of pardon to the penitent, and of Divine assistance to those who labor for progress in moral excellence; by the light which he has thrown on the path of duty; by his own spotless example, in which the loveliness and sublimity of virtue shine forth to warm and quicken, as well as to guide us to perfection; by his threatenings against incorrigible guilt; by his glorious discoveries of immortality; by his sufferings and death; by that signal event, the resurrection, which powerfully bore witness to his Divine mission, and brought down to men's senses a future life; by his continual intercession, which obtains for us spiritual aid and blessings; and by the power with which he is invested, of raising the dead, judging the world, and conferring the everlasting rewards promised to the faithful. . . .

I have thus given the distinguishing views of those Christians in whose names I have spoken. We have embraced this system, not hastily or lightly, but after much deliberation, and we hold it fast, not merely because we believe it to be true, but because we regard it as purifying truth, as a doctrine according to godliness, as able to "work mightily" and to "bring forth fruit" in them that believe. That we wish to spread it, we have no desire to conceal; but we think that we wish its diffusion, because we regard it as more friendly to practical piety and pure morals than the opposite doctrines, because it gives clearer and nobler views of duty, and stronger motives to its performance, because it recommends religion at once to the understanding and the heart, because it asserts the lovely and venerable attributes of God, because it tends to restore the benevolent spirit of Jesus to his divided and afflicted Church, and because it cuts off every hope of God's favor, except that which springs from practical conformity to the life and precepts of Christ. We see nothing in our views to give offence, save their purity, and it is their purity which makes us seek and hope their extension through the world. . . .

In 1820, the year following Channing's sermon, the Massachusetts Supreme Court rendered a decision as important in the sphere of law as "Unitarian Christianity" was in the sphere of theology. This was the famous "Dedham case."

In 1818 the First Church of Dedham, a village southwest of Boston, had divided over the calling of a new minister. The parish (i.e., the adult citizens of the town), having become sympathetic to Unitarianism, called a liberal, the Rev. Alvan Lamson. The church (i.e., those persons who attended regularly), a smaller, more tradition-minded group consisting largely of women, objected to the choice of Mr. Lamson by a vote of fourteen to eighteen. In spite of the church's opposition, the parish settled and ordained Mr. Lamson as its minister. Whereupon the majority of the members of the church, assuming themselves to be the true society, withdrew, claiming as their own the property, furnishings, and records they left behind. When this happened the people of the parish, plus the liberal minority of the church, replaced the former deacons with new deacons of their own number, and sued for the recovery of the church property.

The question for the court to decide was: Which group was the First Church in Dedham and entitled to the property?

The decision was critical for both wings of the Church in Massachusetts. At stake was the property not only of the Dedham church but of every church in the Commonwealth whose membership was divided between liberals and orthodox.

A jury trial was held in February 1820. The jury's decision, directed by Chief Justice Isaac Parker, was handed down the following October. It read: "When the majority of the members of a Congregational church separate from the majority of the parish, the members who remain, although a minority, constitute the church in such parish, and retain the rights and property belonging thereto."

Following are excerpts from the seldom-quoted "Opinion of the Court" in the Dedham case, on which its decision was based.[32]

Hitherto we have gone upon the ground, that at the time when the earliest of these grants were made, there was a body of men in Dedham, known by the name of the Dedham Church; distinct from the society of Christians usually worshipping together in that town. . . . Probably there was no very familiar distinction at that time between the church and the whole assembly of Christians in the town. We have had no evidence that the inhabitants were divided into two bodies, of church and society or parish—keeping separate records, and having separate interests; but if the fact be otherwise than is supposed, there is no doubt that most of the inhabitants of the town were church members at that time. In the year 1631, ten years only before the earliest of these grants, it was provided by a colonial law, that no inhabitants should have the political rights of a free man, unless he were a member of some orthodox church. The presumption is violent then, that almost if not quite all of the adult inhabitants of Dedham and other towns were church members, and a grant to the church, under such circumstances, could mean nothing else than a grant to the town. . . .—That this was the state of things, will not be doubted by those who look into the ancient tracts and writings, respecting the churches in New England. . . .

Considering then that the land granted was for the beneficial use of the assembly of Christians in Dedham, which were no other than the inhabitants of that town who constituted the religious society, within which the church was established, these inhabitants were the *cestui que trusts**—and the equitable title was vested in them, as long as they continued to constitute the assembly denominated the church in the grants.

. . . No particular number is necessary to constitute a church, nor is there any established quorum, which would have a right to manage the concerns of the body. According to the Cambridge platform,† ch. 3, § 4, the number is to be no larger than can conveniently meet together in one place, nor ordinarily fewer than may conveniently carry on church work. It would seem to follow from the very structure of such a body as this, which is a mere voluntary association, that a diminution of its numbers will not affect its identity. A church may exist, in an ecclesiastical sense, without any officers, as will be seen in the platform. . . . The only circumstance therefore, which gives a church any legal character, is its connexion with some regularly constituted society; and those who withdraw from the society cease to be members of that particular church, and the remaining members continue to be the identical church. . . .

We consider then the non-concurrence of the church in the choice of the minister, and in the invitation to the ordaining council, as in no degree impairing the constitutional right of the parish. —That council might have refused to proceed, but the parish could not by that have been deprived of their minister. It was right and proper, as they could not proceed according to ancient usage, because of the dissent of the church, to approach as near to it as possible by calling a respectable council, and having their sanction in the ordination. And it was certainly wise in that council, finding that the points of disagreement were such as would be likely to cause a permanent separation, to yield to the wishes of the parish, and give their sanction to proceedings, which were justified by the constitution and laws of the land. They ordained him over the parish only: but by virtue of that act, founded upon the choice of the people, he became not only the minister of the parish, but of the church still remaining there, notwithstanding the secession of a majority of the members. Mr. Lamson thus became the lawful minister of the first parish in Dedham, and of the church subsisting therein; and he had a right to call church meetings, and do all other acts per-

---

* Beneficiaries of property and funds held by a trustee, i.e., the church—*Ed.*
† The "charter" of Massachusetts Congregationalism, 1648—*Ed.*

taining to a settled and ordained minister of the gospel. The church had a right to choose deacons, finding that the former deacons had abdicated their office; and thus no legal objection is found to exist against their right to maintain this action. . . .

Having established the points necessary to settle this cause, viz. that the property sued for belongs to the first church in Dedham, *sub modo*; that is, to be managed by its deacons under the superintendance of the church, for the general good of the inhabitants of the first parish, in the support of the publick worship of God:—that the members of the church, now associated and worshipping with the first parish, constitute the first church:—and that the plaintiffs are duly appointed deacons of that church; it follows that the verdict of the jury is right, and that judgment must be entered accordingly.

The Dedham case rocked Massachusetts Congregationalism to its foundation. Many ministers could not believe it. More were shocked and embittered. Some of the orthodox accused Judge Parker of bias because he was himself a Unitarian.

The withdrawal of Trinitarians from the Unitarian-dominated churches to form new societies, and vice versa to a much smaller extent, proceeded rapidly. Within twenty years one-quarter of the 544 Congregational churches in Massachusetts were Unitarian. With the Unitarians claiming most of the leading ministers and laity, one observer later said that the Massachusetts churches had "blown their brains out."

The Unitarian cause took another forward stride in 1821 with the establishment of a weekly newspaper in Boston, the Christian Register. It was not the first Unitarian periodical—others dated back to 1805—but it was the first with a popular purpose and audience. Today as a monthly it is the oldest religious journal of continuous publication in America.

The Register's mission was outlined in the first editorial by its founder and editor, David Reed, in Volume 1, Number 1, April 20, 1821.[33]

TO THE PUBLIC

The present period is distinguished above any other since the first settlement of our country, for the general prevalence of a spirit of free religious inquiry. Amongst all classes of the community, there has been discovered of late, an increasing desire to understand better, and to bring into practical exercise, the genuine principles and spirit of Christianity. And it is with much satisfaction, that the friends of enlightened piety have perceived, that whilst this spirit of inquiry has been exercised with a considerable degree of freedom and boldness, it has, at the same time, been so effectually guarded by good sense, and chastened by piety, that the cause of truth, instead of suffering detriment, has been greatly promoted, by the light that has been thrown upon the true doctrines and principles of our religion.

It will, however, no doubt, be generally admitted that something remains still to be done, to increase the purity of our Christian faith, and to promote its genuine practical influence upon the heart and life. It seems important, not only that the spirit of inquiry that is abroad, should be kept alive, but that exertions be made, to assist and guide the inquiries of those who are honestly seeking the truth. This important purpose, has been indeed, already essentially promoted, by that valuable periodical work, the *Christian Disciple*. But, considering the high literary character of this work, and that it is issued only once in two months, it has been thought expedient that the public be furnished with a weekly religious newspaper.

The subscriber proposes, therefore, to publish weekly in Boston, the CHRISTIAN REGISTER, a work, which, in its doctrines and temper, shall harmonize with the Christian Disciple, but which shall be more elementary, and better adapted to the taste and wants of those whose advantages of reading and inquiry have been less extensive. The great object of the Christian Register will be to inculcate the principles of a rational faith, and to promote the practice of genuine piety. To accomplish this purpose, it will aim to excite a spirit of free and independent religious inquiry, and to assist in ascertaining and bringing into use, the true principles of interpreting the scriptures. It will urge the importance and duty of subjecting our faith to the test of scripture and enlightened reason, and of rejecting from our creed, not only what is contrary to the general language of the scriptures, but every thing that is not plainly and explicitly taught there. It will also enforce the duty, of a serious and practical regard, to the moral precepts of Christianity, by showing that the final favour of God toward us, is to depend not so much upon what has been done to us or for us by another, as upon the temper of mind we have ourselves cherished, and the course of moral conduct we have pursued. And it will earnestly recommend to all, the cultivation of the mild and amiable spirit of the gospel toward those who differ from them, from the belief that genuine piety is not confined to any sect, but exists in a greater or less degree amongst all, and that he is the best Christian, not whose speculations are in nearest accordance with the faith of the majority, but whose life and temper are most perfectly and habitually under the influence of the precepts and spirit of the gospel.

It is believed that a work of this kind, if conducted with ability and candor, might render an important service to the cause of truth, piety and Christian love, by diffusing religious knowledge, by giving enlargement and catholicism to the views and feelings of men, and by inculcating those true and rational principles of religion, which are so important to our virtue and happiness.

In conducting this work, in a manner that shall render it an instructive, entertaining and useful publication, the subscriber would inform the public, that he does not rely wholly upon his own strength and resources. He has the promise of the patronage, counsel, and occasional assistance, of a number of gentlemen in this town and vicinity, who stand high in the estimation of the public, for their scientific and theological acquirements, as well as for the soundness of their religious principles. To render the work, as far as possible, satisfactory to subscribers, each number shall contain a summary of the important foreign and domestic news, both political and miscellaneous.—Political discussions, however, shall never be admitted.

The Theological department shall contain articles original and extracted, on various subjects, doctrinal, critical and practical, with occasional biography and poetry and sketches of ecclesiastical history. It shall also contain such well authenticated intelligence as may be obtained, respecting the moral and religious state of different parts of the world, with accounts of the character, operations and success, of the various societies and institutions, in this and other countries, for moral and benevolent purposes.

It is hoped, that the subscribers for this work, will find it sufficiently valuable, to induce them to preserve a regular series of the different numbers. At the close of each year a copious index will be furnished of the subjects treated during the preceding year. This will enable those who preserve a series of the numbers, to turn with ease to any subject that may have been treated, and thus to revive the recollection of whatever is interesting or important in the communications of the year.

DAVID REED

While the Unitarian controversy raged in New England, a solitary liberal lived out his days in Charlottesville, Virginia. Thomas Jefferson devoted the last years of his life to gathering the University of Virginia, managing his estate at Monticello, and to writing and correspondence. Events made him hopeful for the future of America and of Unitarianism. In June 1822 he wrote:[34]

Had the doctrines of Jesus been preached always as pure as they came from his lips, the whole civilized world would now have been Christian. I rejoice that in this blessed country of free inquiry and belief, which has surrendered its conscience to neither kings nor priests, the genuine doctrine of only one God is reviving, and I trust that there is not a young man now living in the United States who will not die a Unitarian.

Later the same year he wrote to a correspondent in Ohio:[35]

Sir,—I have to thank you for your pamphlets on the subject of Unitarianism, and to express my gratification with your efforts for the revival of primitive Christianity in your quarter. No historical fact is better established, than that the doctrine of one God, pure and uncompounded, was that of the early ages of Christianity; and was among the efficacious doctrines which gave it triumph over the polytheism of the ancients, sickened with the absurdities of their own theology. Nor was the unity of the Supreme Being ousted from the Christian creed by the force of reason, but by the sword of civil government, wielded at the will of the fanatic Athanasius. The hocus-pocus phantasm of a God like another Cerberus, with one body and three heads, had its birth and growth in the blood of thousands and thousands of martyrs. And a strong proof of the solidity of the primitive faith, is its restoration, as soon as a nation arises which vindicates to itself the freedom of religious opinion, and its external divorce from the civil authority. The pure and simple unity of the Creator of the universe, is now all but ascendant in the Eastern States; it is dawning in the West, and advancing towards the South; and I confidently expect that the present generation will see Unitarianism become the general religion of the United States. . . .

Jefferson imagined Unitarianism sweeping irresistibly across the country. He took it for granted that all who encountered its "pure and simple doctrine" would be converted, and that orthodoxy would quickly fade away. He was mistaken.

One obstacle to Unitarian growth was aggressive organizing by other denominations. A second obstacle was the lack of organization among Unitarians who, as the Register commented, "make but very little use of the advantages of coalition or united effort, for inculcating their peculiar sentiments." A third obstacle was hinted at by Jefferson when he wrote, "I know there are many around me who would gladly become so [i.e., Unitarian], if once they could hear the questions fairly stated." The Unitarians were unwilling to employ missionaries. Channing feared that a Unitarian missionary program would heighten antagonisms between Unitarians and Congregationalists. Many Unitarians dismissed missionary work as being beneath their social rank.

The younger generation was not so cautious, however. A group of young Harvard Divinity graduates had for several years discussed ways of advancing the Unitarian cause through organization. By 1824 the idea had progressed so far that the Anonymous Association, a conversation club of which 'Channing was a leading member, discussed "the practicality and expediency of forming a Unitarian convention or association, to consist of clergymen and laymen, to meet annually or oftener." The discussion was favorable, a committee was appointed, and a general meeting called on January 27, 1825 to consider a plan of organization. Forty-four Massachusetts ministers and laity attended. The minutes of this meeting, written by the Rev. James Walker, are published here for the first time exactly as recorded.[36]

Boston, January 27, 1825

The meeting was organised by choosing Hon Richard Sullivan Moderator. & Mr Jas. Walker Secretary.

Prayers were offered by Revd Dr Channing.

A communication was read by Rev Dr Ware [Henry Ware the younger], containing some exposition of the objects of this meeting, which concluded by proposing the two following resolutions.

(1st) It is desirable and expedient that provision should now be made for future meetings of the Unitarians and liberal Christians generally.

(2) That a committee consisting of [9] members be appointed to consider with what degree of frequency such shall be held,—& to form a plan upon which they shall be conducted; to report to this body at an adjourned meeting.

It was moved by Mr Higginson that the first resolution be adopted by the meeting. The motion was seconded.

The debate was opened by Rev. Dr Bancroft [of Worcester] who was fearful that sufficient care might not be taken in the manner of instituting the meetings proposed. He considered that Unitarianism was to be propagated slowly and silently. It had been so from the beginning in the progress of Unitarians in this country. Did not wish to oppose the design generally.

Professor [Andrews] Norton [of Harvard Divinity School] followed. The object of the association was not to make proselytes, or he should be opposed to it. His experience was in favour of associations. He instanced its effects, & good effects, in the eyes of the Quakers and Methodists.

The meeting was next addressed by Rev. Dr Channing. Did not agree with the gentleman who spoke last. Thought the object of the association, or as he preferred it should be the Convention, to spread our views òf religion; not our mere opinions, for our religion is essentially practical. The convention should bring together gentlemen from every part of the country to compare [?] their views, & ascertain the wants of different places. Tendencies were good, but an association would give them effects.

Judge Jackson [of the Massachusetts Supreme Court] followed. Was altogether opposed to the project. Thought it was not becoming to ourselves, nor consistent with our principles, nor beneficial to the community. We can do any thing that is necessary without such a general association for all purposes. Was ready to unite for any specified purpose if any such purpose could be presented.

Followed by Mr [Jared] Sparks. Advocated the measure. Thought it our duty to aid the cause of which we consider the truth. Necessary to promote sympathy among the Unitarians throughout the country.

Rev. Dr. Pierce [of Brookline] opposed the measure, as very dangerous. Likely to be unpopular in 75 liberal parishes in the interiors of the State. Would be very dangerous to him.

Revd Mr Edes. Was very much in favour of the projected association. Considered it necessary for the support of distant parishes by way of sympathy.

Dr Pierce rose again and asserted his views. Parishes in the country [are] composed of all sorts of Christians: of course some would be unfavourably affected.

Mr Bradford stated that Gentlemen from a distance invited to attend this meeting but unable, had answered the Committee's invitation approving the object. Approved the object himself [;] thought more discussion proper among Unitarians at the present day.

Professor Norton thought Unitarians had not protected & fostered the Institutions under their care. Theo. School. Evang. Miss. Soc. Unison necessary to mutual excitement in effecting these objects.

Mr Lewis Tappan. Favoured the association. Necessary to make Unitarians acquainted with [one] another: No member connected with Association pledged to anything done in it. May leave at any time.

Mr George Bond [Boston merchant]. Believed the measure inexpedient under existing circumstances: Was afraid that U[nitarians]. would become the majority in this country. When they would act as other majorities have acted. Admitted that U[nitarians]. had not done as much as they should for benevolent objects. Concluded by moving an adjournment to the day before the next Commencement. (not seconded.)

Rev. Dr. Abbot [of Beverly]. Stated that Dr Fisher & others in a conversation with him were opposed to the party association. Unitarians in his neighborhood owed everything to slow & silent progress[.] Thought presenting a distinct object for opposition would arrest the progress of U.

Rev Dr Allyn [of Duxbury] averse to the measure. Opposed to taking any name; especially Unitarian or Liberal can be made of any use by opponents. Thought the Christians wise in not having a name. Thought a loose convention might be formed. Should be happy to meet a delegation of all sects. Should wish some such turn should be given to this association should it go into operation.

Rev. Mr Harding of New Salem. Society's in his neighborhood had been obliged to take ground. Trinitarians no longer mixed up with Unitarians. Would like an Association for practical purposes. Opposed a mere sectarian association.

A Letter from Mr Williard was read approving the object.

Mr Dwight of Springfield. Said Mr Howard favoured the object. Favoured it himself. Thought the objection directed against the abuse of it of no weight. Thought we ought not distrust ourselves. We should go on with as good purposes as we begin with.

Revd Mr [John] Pierpont. Gave the opinion of Mr Atherton of Amherst in favour of the measure. Thought himself that it was reassuring to the support of a Society in the Country like that in Amherst. Important to have preaching in the country in various places, which the people will attend—Like Methodists Camp Meetings—Conferences. Thought all strong action particular action—sectional action, sectarian action. Was willing to bear the name U. We could not divest ourselves of it. Thought the general interest of U. should be at the same time promoted.

Mr Higginson. Dr Thayer & Mr May were in favour of it. The late efforts of Unitarians alluded to by Judge Jackson proofs in favour of association. New Ch[urche]s & Theolog. Schools, owed every thing to the zeal & efforts of a few Unitarians who had associated together, and acted in such association.

Rev Dr Pierce considered the absense of gentlemen from a distance an argument for its not being wished for by them.

Mr Tappan. Accounted for their absense & showed that the absense of all the gentlemen invited, could be accounted for without authorising any such inference. The Committee stated again that most of those invited & who were unable to attend had answered their letters approving generally the object.

Rev. Mr Bigelow opposed. Would not promote union nor interests of U. Said that Gov. Brooks thought no other exertions need be made.

Letter from Gov. Brooks was read.

Moved by Mr Norton that a Committee be appointed to invite a larger number of gentlemen sometime during the next session of general Court. Seconded and passed.

Voted that the Committee consist of nine, to fill their own vacancies should any, who were elected, decline[.]

Voted that the three gentlemen, viz. Hon. Richard Sullivan, Rev Dr Ware and Mr Alden Bradford who sent out the letter for this meeting constitute three of the nine and that to these be added Dr Channing Mr Higginson Mr Walker—Mr Pierpont Mr Palfrey —Mr Bradford[.]

Judge Howes Letter approving the objects & Letter of Rev Dr Nichols approving the objects were read.

Adjourned.

Because of the division of opinion over the proposal to organize a Unitarian association, the contemplated meeting was never held. But the young ministers, led by Walker, Henry Ware, Jr., and Ezra S. Gannett, were undaunted. Four months later, on May 25, they presented their plan for an Association to the Berry Street Conference of ministers in Boston, where it was well received. The next day, May 26, 1825, the American Unitarian Association was formed "to diffuse the knowledge and promote the interests of pure Christianity."

The formation of the American Unitarian Association marked the final separation of Unitarians from Congregationalists. Henceforth they were two denominations. The American Unitarian Association's main activities consisted of sponsoring publications and travelling "agents." Within a decade the movement had spread westward, with new churches in Buffalo, Chicago, St. Louis, New Orleans, and a half dozen other cities. The Unitarian controversy among the Congregationalists thus was ended. A new phase of the controversy, which was to divide Unitarian from Unitarian, and ultimately become "the most striking intellectual movement in the history of America," was shortly to begin—Transcendentalism.

Ralph Waldo Emerson (1803-1882), the leading spirit of Transcendentalism, began life, like his contemporary Channing, as a small, frail, sternly disciplined child. Unlike Channing, Emerson came from a family of ministers. On graduating from Harvard he taught school briefly, then entered the Unitarian ministry at Second

Church in Boston. His temperament was such, however, that he found church work cold and restrictive, and he resigned after two years to lecture and write.

His search for a satisfying meaning in life led him to Europe in 1832-1833 where he encountered the philosophies of idealism and Romanticism. From these he became convinced that God resides not in formal religion but in Nature, not in rites but in persons. "I grow in God," he wrote in 1837, "I am only a form of him. He is the soul of me. I can even with a mountainous aspiring say, I am God." Thus Emerson came to regard spirit, or soul, as the fundamental reality, the source of life, reverence, virtue.

In March 1838 Emerson, now a well-known litterateur, accepted the invitation of the Senior Class of the Harvard Divinity School to deliver "the customary discourse, on occasion of their entering upon the active Christian ministry." The following July 15 he rose in the chapel of Divinity Hall to present to an unsuspecting audience his "Divinity School Address." [37]

In this refulgent summer, it has been a luxury to draw the breath of life. The grass grows, the buds burst, the meadow is spotted with fire and gold in the tint of flowers. The air is full of birds, and sweet with the breath of the pine, the balm-of-Gilead, and the new hay. Night brings no gloom to the heart with its welcome shade. Through the transparent darkness the stars pour their almost spiritual rays. Man under them seems a young child, and his huge globe a toy. The cool night bathes the world as with a river, and prepares his eyes again for the crimson dawn. The mystery of nature was never displayed more happily. . . . One is constrained to respect the perfection of this world in which our senses converse. How wide; how rich; what invitation from every property it gives to every faculty of man! In its fruitful soils; in its navigable sea; in its mountains of metal and stone; in its forests of all woods; in its animals; in its chemical ingredients; in the powers and path of light, heat, attraction and life, it is well worth the pith and heart of great men to subdue and enjoy it. . . .

But when the mind opens, and reveals the laws which traverse the universe and make things what they are, then shrinks the great world at once into a mere illusion and fable of this mind. What am I? and What is? asks the human spirit with a curiosity new-kindled, but never to be quenched. Behold these outrunning laws, which our imperfect apprehension can see tend this way and that, but not come full circle. Behold these infinite relations, so like, so unlike; many, yet one. I would study, I would know, I would admire forever. These works of thought have been the entertainments of the human spirit in all ages.

A more secret, sweet, and overpowering beauty appears to man when his heart and mind open to the sentiment of virtue. . . .

The sentiment of virtue is a reverence and delight in the presence of certain divine laws. It perceives that this homely game of life we play, covers, under what seem foolish details, principles that astonish. The child amidst his baubles is learning the action of light, motion, gravity, muscular force; and in the game of human life, love, fear, justice, appetite, man, and God, interact. These laws refuse to be adequately stated. They will not be written out on paper, or spoken by the tongue. They elude our persevering thought; yet we read them hourly in each other's faces, in each other's actions, in our own remorse. The moral traits which are all globed into every virtuous act and thought,—in speech we must sever, and describe or suggest by painful enumeration of many particulars. Yet, as this sentiment is the essence of all religion, let me guide your eye to the precise objects of the sentiment, by an enumeration of some of those classes of facts in which this element is conspicuous.

The intuition of the moral sentiment is an insight of the perfection of the laws of the soul. These laws execute themselves. They are out of time, out of space, and not subject to circumstance. Thus in the soul of man there is a justice whose retributions are instant and entire. He who does a good deed is instantly ennobled, He who does a mean deed is by the action itself contracted. He who puts off impurity, thereby puts on purity. If a man is at heart just, then in so far is he God; the safety of God, the immortality of God, the majesty of God, do enter into that man with justice. If a man dissemble, deceive, he deceives himself, and goes out of acquaintance with his own being. A man in the view of absolute goodness, adores, with total humility. Every step so downward, is a step upward. The man who renounces himself, comes to himself. . . .

The perception of this law of laws awakens in the mind a sentiment which we call the religious sentiment, and which makes our highest happiness. . . .

This sentiment is divine and deifying. It is the beatitude of man. It makes him illimitable. Through it, the soul first knows itself. It corrects the capital mistake of the infant man, who seeks to be great by following the great, and hopes to derive advantages from another,—by showing the fountain of all good to be in himself, and that he, equally with every man, is an inlet into the deeps of Reason. When he says, "I ought"; when love warms him; when he chooses, warned from on high, the good and great deed; then, deep melodies wander through his soul from Supreme Wisdom. Then he can worship, and be enlarged by his worship; for he can never go behind this sentiment. In the sublimest flights of the soul, rectitude is never surmounted, love is never outgrown.

This sentiment lies at the foundation of society, and successively creates all forms of worship. The principle of veneration never dies out. Man fallen into superstition, into sensuality, is never quite without the visions of the moral sentiment. In like manner, all the expressions of this sentiment are sacred and permanent in proportion to their purity. The expressions of this sentiment affect us more than all other compositions. The sentences of the oldest time, which ejaculate this piety, are still fresh and fragrant. This thought dwelled always deepest in the minds of men in the devout and contemplative East; not alone in Palestine, where it reached its purest expression, but in Egypt, in Persia, in India, in China. Europe has always owed to oriental genius its divine impulses. What these holy bards said, all sane men found agreeable and true. And the unique impression of Jesus upon mankind, whose name is not so much written as ploughed into the history of this world, is proof of the subtle virtue of this infusion.

Meantime, whilst the doors of the temple stand open, night and day, before every man, and the oracles of this truth cease never, it is guarded by one stern condition; this namely; it is an intuition. It cannot be received at second hand. Truly speaking, it is not instruction, but provocation, that I can receive from another soul. What he announces, I must find true in me, or wholly reject, and on his word, or as his second, be he who he may, I can accept nothing. On the contrary, the absence of this primary faith is the presence of degradation. As is the flood so is the ebb. Let this faith depart, and the very words it spake and the things it made become false and hurtful. Then falls the church, the state, art, letters, life.

The doctrine of the divine nature being forgotten, a sickness infects and dwarfs the constitution. Once man was all; now he is an appendage, a nuisance. And because the indwelling Supreme Spirit cannot wholly be got rid of, the doctrine of it suffers this perversion, that the divine nature is attributed to one or two persons, and denied to all the rest. . . .

Jesus Christ belonged to the true race of prophets. He saw with open eye the mystery of the soul. Drawn by its severe harmony, ravished with its beauty, he lived in it, and had his being there. Alone in all history he estimated the greatness of man. One man was true to what is in you and me. He saw that God incarnates himself in man, and evermore goes forth anew to take possession of his World. He said in this jubilee of sublime emotion, "I am divine. Through me, God acts; through me speaks. Would you see God, see me; or see thee, when thou also thinkest as I now think." But what a distortion did his doctrine and memory suffer in the same, in the next, and the following ages! There is no doctrine of the Reason which will bear to be taught by the Understanding. The understanding caught this high chant from the poet's lips, and said, in the next age, "This was Jehovah come down out of heaven. I will kill you, if you say he was a man." The idioms of his language and the figures of his rhetoric have usurped the place of his truth; and churches are not built on his principles, but on his tropes [i.e., figures of speech]. Christianity became a Mythus, as the poetic teaching of Greece and of Egypt, before. He spoke of miracles; for he felt that man's life was a miracle, and all that man doth, and he knew that this daily miracle shines as the character ascends. But the word Miracle, as pronounced by Christian churches, gives a false impression; it is Monster. It is not one with the blowing clover and the falling rain. . . .

. . . Historic Christianity has fallen into the error that corrupts all attempts to communicate religion. As it appears to us, and as it has appeared for ages, it is not the doctrine of the soul, but an exaggeration of the personal, the positive, the ritual. It has dwelt, it dwells, with noxious exaggeration about the person of Jesus. The soul knows no persons. It invites every man to expand to the full circle of the universe, and will have no preferences but those of spontaneous love. . . .

That is always best which gives me to myself. The su
excited in me by the great stoical doctrine, Obey thyself. That
which shows God in me, fortifies me. That which shows God out
of me, makes me a wart and a wen. There is no longer a necessary
reason for my being. Already the long shadows of untimely oblivion
creep over me, and I shall decease forever.

. . . The time is coming when all men will see that the gift of
God to the soul is not a vaunting, overpowering, excluding sanctity,
but a sweet, natural goodness, a goodness like thine and mine, and
that so invites thine and mine to be and to grow. . . .

The second defect of the traditionary and limited way of using
the mind of Christ, is a consequence of the first; this, namely; that
the Moral Nature, that Law of laws whose revelations introduce
greatness,—yea, God himself,—into the open soul, is not explored
as the fountain of the established teaching in society. Men have
come to speak of the revelation as somewhat long ago given and
done, as if God were dead. . . .

. . . The spirit only can teach. Not any profane man, not any
sensual, not any liar, not any slave can teach, but only he can give,
who has; he only can create, who is. The man on whom the soul
descends, through whom the soul speaks, alone can teach. Courage,
piety, love, wisdom, can teach; and every man can open his door
to these angels, and they shall bring him the gift of tongues. But
the man who aims to speak as books enable, as synods use, as the
fashion guides, and as interest commands, babbles. Let him hush.

And now, my brothers, you will ask, What in these desponding
days can be done by us? The remedy is already declared in the
ground of our complaint of the Church. We have contrasted the
Church with the Soul. In the soul then let the redemption be
sought. Wherever a man comes, there comes revolution. The old
is for slaves. When a man comes, all books are legible, all things
transparent, all religions are forms. He is religious. Man is the
wonder-worker. He is seen amid miracles. All men bless and curse.
He saith yea and nay, only. The stationariness of religion; the as-
sumption that the age of inspiration is past, that the Bible is closed;
the fear of degrading the character of Jesus by representing him as
a man;—indicate with sufficient clearness the falsehood of our theology. It is the office of a true teacher to show us that God *is*, not

was; that he speaketh, not spake. . . . Yourself a new-born bard of
the Holy Ghost, cast behind you all conformity, and acquaint men
at first hand with Deity. . . .

. . . The question returns, What shall we do? I confess, all attempts to project and establish a Cultus with new rites and forms,
seem to me vain. Faith makes us, and not we it, and faith makes
its own forms. All attempts to contrive a system are as cold as the
new worship introduced by the French to the goddess of Reason,—
to-day, pasteboard and filigree, and ending to-morrow in madness and
murder. Rather let the breath of new life be breathed by you
through the forms already existing. For if once you are alive, you
shall find they shall become plastic and new. The remedy to their
deformity is first, soul, and second, soul, and evermore, soul. The
whole popedom of forms one pulsation of virtue can uplift and
vivify. Two inestimable advantages Christianity has given us: first,
the Sabbath, the jubilee of the whole world, whose light dawns
welcome alike into the closet of the philosopher, into the garret of
toil, and into prison-cells, and everywhere suggests, even to the vile,
the dignity of spiritual being. Let it stand forevermore, a temple,
which new love, new faith, new sight shall restore to more than its
first splendor to mankind. And secondly, the institution of preaching,
—the speech of man to men,—essentially the most flexible of all
organs, of all forms. What hinders that now, everywhere, in pulpits,
in lecture-rooms, in houses, in fields, wherever the invitation of men
or your own occasions lead you, you speak the very truth, as your
life and conscience teach it, and cheer the waiting, fainting hearts
of men with new hope and new revelation?

I look for the hour when that supreme Beauty which ravished
the souls of those eastern men, and chiefly of those Hebrews, and
through their lips spoke oracles to all time, shall speak in the West
also. . . . I look for the new Teacher that shall follow so far those
shining laws that he shall see them come full circle; shall see their
rounding complete grace; shall see the world to be the mirror of the
soul; shall see the identity of the law of gravitation with purity of
heart; and shall show that the Ought, that Duty, is one thing with
Science, with Beauty, and with Joy.

*In an hour and a half Emerson had in effect demolished what had
taken eighteen centuries to build and maintain—the authority of*

Christian faith based on the miracles of Jesus. The reaction was instantaneous and far-reaching. Professor Andrews Norton wrote an open letter to a Boston newspaper expressing the "disgust and strong disapprobation" with which the Divinity faculty had heard Emerson, and a year later answered him in A Discourse on the Latest Form of Infidelity. The Christian Examiner said that, to most Unitarian ministers, Emerson's notions were "neither good divinity nor good sense." Orestes Brownson's Boston Quarterly Review thought the address "somewhat arrogant" but predicted that Emerson's "free spirit, and free utterance" would exert a lasting effect on American literature. To Theodore Parker, the young minister in West Roxbury, Massachusetts, the address was "the noblest and most inspiring strain I ever listened to."

Parker (1810-1860) was in many ways the most remarkable leader produced by the Unitarian movement in America. Grandson of Lexington's Captain John Parker, who said of the British in 1775, "If they mean to have a war, let it begin here," Theodore threw down the same challenge to the theological and economic royalists of his day. An intellectual giant, a commanding preacher, an "emancipator" second only to Abraham Lincoln in stature and influence, Parker lived and died as the conscience of American Unitarianism.

Educated in Lexington by tutors, he taught school before entering Harvard Divinity School. The foremost influence on his early theology was the Biblical criticism of the Germans DeWette, Schleiermacher, and Baur, who sought to understand Jesus as a figure in history.

Parker's ministry began in West Roxbury, where he was in close touch with his former teachers, the best libraries, and the intellectual ferment in and around Boston. To his congregation he resolved "to preach nothing as religion that I have not experienced inwardly and made my own." Here he ministered to his seventy families, wrote articles for Transcendentalist journals, and conversed with fellow reformers at Brook Farm.

Emerson's Divinity School Address had thrilled Parker but it had also troubled him, for Emerson had left the church to press his reformation. Was it necessary that he, Parker, do the same? He decided it was not; he would reform the church from within. In pursuit of a purified Christianity he spoke out at the ordination service of Charles C. Shackford, on May 19, 1841 in South Boston, taking as his theme "The Transient and Permanent in Christianity." [38]

"Heaven and earth shall pass away; but my words shall not pass away."—Luke xxi, 33.

In this sentence we have a very clear indication that Jesus of Nazareth believed the religion he taught would be eternal, that the substance of it would last for ever. . . .

Let us look at this matter a little more closely. In actual Christianity—that is, in that portion of Christianity which is preached and believed—there seems to have been, ever since the time of its earthly founder, two elements, the one transient, the other permanent. The one is the thought, the folly, the uncertain wisdom, the theological notions, the impiety of man; the other, the eternal truth of God. These two bear, perhaps, the same relation to each other that the phenomena of outward nature, such as sunshine and cloud, growth, decay, and reproduction, bear to the great law of nature, which underlies and supports them all. As in that case more attention is commonly paid to the particular phenomena than to the general law, so in this case more is generally given to the transient in Christianity than to the permanent therein. . . .

. . . Now there can be but one religion which is absolutely true, existing in the facts of human nature and the ideas of Infinite God. That, whether acknowledged or not, is always the same thing, and never changes. So far as a man has any real religion—either the principle or the sentiment thereof so far he has that, by whatever name he may call it. For, strictly speaking, there is but one kind of religion, as there is but one kind of love, though the manifestations of this religion, in forms, doctrines, and life, be never so diverse. It is through these men approximate to the true expression of this religion. Now, while this religion is one and always the same thing, there may be numerous systems of theology or philosophies of religion. These, with their creeds, confessions, and collections of doctrines, deduced by reasoning upon the facts observed, may be baseless and false, either because the observation was too narrow in extent, or otherwise defective in point of accuracy, or because the reasoning was illogical, and therefore the deduction spurious. Each of these faults is conspicuous in the systems of theology. Now the solar system as it exists in fact is permanent, though the notions of Thales and Ptolemy, of Copernicus and Descartes, about this system, prove transient, imperfect approximations to the true expression. So the Christianity of Jesus is permanent, though what passes for Christianity with popes and catechisms, with sects and churches, in the first century or in the nineteenth century, prove transient also. . . .

To turn away from the disputes of the Catholics and the Protestants, of the Unitarian and the Trinitarian, of old school and new school, and come to the plain words of Jesus of Nazareth, Christianity is a simple thing, very simple. It is absolute, pure morality; absolute, pure religion; the love of man; the love of God acting without let or hindrance. The only creed it lays down is the great truth which springs up spontaneous in the holy heart—there is a God. Its watchword is, Be perfect as your Father in heaven. The only form it demands is a divine life; doing the best thing in the best way, from the highest motives; perfect obedience to the great law of God. Its sanction is the voice of God in your heart; the perpetual presence of him who made us and the stars over our head; Christ and the Father abiding within us. All this is very simple— a little child can understand it; very beautiful—the loftiest mind can find nothing so lovely. Try it by reason, conscience, and faith— things highest in man's nature we see no redundance, we feel no deficiency. Examine the particular duties it enjoins—humility, reverence, sobriety, gentleness, charity, forgiveness, fortitude, resignation, faith, and active love; try the whole extent of Christianity, so well summed up in the command, "Thou shalt love the Lord thy God with all thy heart, and with all thy soul, and with all thy mind— thou shalt love thy neighbor as thyself," and is there anything therein that can perish? No, the very opponents of Christianity have rarely found fault with the teachings of Jesus. The end of Christianity seems to be to make all men one with God as Christ was one with him; to bring them to such a state of obedience and goodness that we shall think divine thoughts and feel divine sentiments, and so keep the law of God by living a life of truth and love. Its means are purity and prayer; getting strength from God, and using it for our fellow-men as well as ourselves. It allows perfect freedom. It does not demand all men to think alike, but to think uprightly, and get as near as possible at truth; not all men to live alike, but to live holy, and get as near as possible to a life perfectly divine . . . for Christianity is not a system of doctrines, but rather a method of attaining oneness with God. It demands, therefore, a good life of piety within, of purity without, and gives the promise that whoso does God's will shall know of God's doctrine. . . .

. . . God send us a real religious life, which shall pluck blindness out of the heart, and make us better fathers, mothers, and children! a religious life, that shall go with us where we go, and make every home the house of God, every act acceptable as a prayer. We would work for this, and pray for it, though we wept tears of blood while we prayed.

Such, then, is the transient and such the permanent in Christianity. What is of absolute value never changes; we may cling round it and grow to it for ever. No one can say his notions shall stand. But we may all say, the truth as it is in Jesus shall never pass away. Yet there are always some, even religious men, who do not see the permanent element, so they rely on the fleeting, and, what is also an evil, condemn others for not doing the same. They mistake a defence of the truth for an attack upon the holy of holies, the removal of a theological error for the destruction of all religion. Already men of the same sect eye one another with suspicion, and lowering brows indicate a storm, and, like children who have fallen out in their play, call hard names. Now, as always, there is a collision between these two elements. The question puts itself to each man, "Will you cling to what is perishing, or embrace what is eternal?" This question each must answer for himself. . . . Choose as you will choose; but weal or woe depends upon your choice.

Parker later described the reaction to his sermon. "The Trinitarian ministers who were present joined in a public protest; a great outcry was raised against the sermon and its author . . . 'Unbeliever,' 'infidel,' 'atheist,' were the titles bestowed on me by my brothers in the Christian ministry. . . ." Henceforth Parker was an outcast: few ministers would exchange pulpits with him, and one who did lost fifteen of his leading families. The reason was not that all the ministers disagreed with his doctrines, for many were as heretical as he, but that through associating with him they would become outcasts too.

The exclusion of Parker from friendly society was intensified by his opposition to the "respectable" evils of his day, especially pov-

erty, war, and slavery. *Piety was not enough—Christianity must
liberate humanity from oppression!* In his "Experience as a Minister"
he wrote, "We need the great charity that palliates effects of wrong,
and the greater justice which removes the cause." In the battle
against slavery, it must be noted, Parker was joined by all but a few
of his ministerial colleagues.

Heretic and reformer—this was Parker. His life as a husband
("I can do nothing without Lydia—not even read") and friend of
children is less well known, but was that which made his public
life tolerable. In 1851 Parker, now the minister of the Twenty-
Eighth Congregational Society which met in the Melodeon (later in
Boston's Music Hall), addressed a meeting of the Boston ministers
on the subject of the Fugitive Slave Law requiring northerners to
turn over runaway slaves to the government so they could be returned
to their masters. His remarks reveal his feelings about slavery, about
himself, and about his fellow ministers who condemned him.[39]

Mr. Gannett [the Rev. Ezra Stiles Gannett, Channing's successor
at Federal Street Church] in demanding obedience to the Fugitive
Slave Law [has] made two points, namely: if it be not obeyed, first
we shall violate all human laws; and next, there will be a dissolution
of the Union.

Let me say a word of each. But first let me say that I attribute
no unmanly motive to Mr. Gannett. I thought him honest when
he denied that I was; I think him honest now. I know him to be
conscientious, laborious, and self-denying . . . if there be any men
in this Conference who honor and esteem Dr. Gannett, I trust I
am second to none of them. But I do not share his opinions or
partake of his fears. His arguments for obeying the Fugitive Slave
Law (ab inconvenienti) I think are of no value.

If we do not obey this law, he says, we shall disobey all laws. It
is not so. There is not a country in the world where there is more
respect for human laws than in New England; nowhere more than
in Massachusetts. . . .

Why are we thus loyal to law? First, because we make the laws
ourselves, and for ourselves; and next, because the laws actually represent the conscience of the people, and help them keep the laws
of God. The value of human laws is only this—to conserve the

great eternal law of God; to enable us to keep that; to hinder us from disobeying that. So long as laws do this we should obey them. . . .

But the Fugitive Slave Law is one which contradicts the acknowledged precepts of the Christian religion, universally acknowledged. It violates the noblest instincts of humanity; it asks us to trample on the law of God. It commands what nature, religion, and God alike forbid; it forbids what nature, religion, and God alike command. It tends to defeat the object of all just human law; it tends to annihilate the observance of the law of God. So faithful to God, to religion, to human nature, and in the name of law itself, we protest against this particular statute, and trample it under our feet.

Who is it that oppose the Fugitive Slave Law? Men that have always been on the side of "law and order," and do not violate the statutes of men for their own advantage. This disobedience to the Fugitive Slave Law is one of the strongest guarantees for the observance of any just law. You cannot trust a people who will keep law; because it is law; nor need we distrust a people that will only keep a law when it is just. The Fugitive Slave Law, if obeyed, will do more to overturn the power of human law, than all disobedience to it—the most complete.

Then as to the dissolution of the Union . . . suppose that was the alternative: that we must have the Fugitive Slave Law, or dissolution. Which were the worst; which comes nearest to the law of God which we all are to keep? . . . For my own part, I would rather see my own house burnt to the ground, and my family thrown, one by one, amid the blazing rafters of my own roof, and I myself be thrown in last of all, rather than have a single fugitive slave sent back as Thomas Sims was sent back. Nay, I should rather see this Union "dissolved" till there was not a territory so large as the county of Suffolk! Let us lose everything but fidelity to God. . . .

A little while ago we were told we must not preach on this matter of slavery, because it was "an abstraction;" then because the North was "all right on that subject;" and then because we had "nothing to do with it," we "must go to Charleston or New Orleans to see it." But now it is a most concrete thing. We see what public opinion is on the matter of slavery; what it is in Boston; nay, what it is with members of this Conference. It favors slavery and this wicked law! We need not go to Charleston and New Orleans to see slavery; our own court-house was a barracoon; our officers of this city were slave-hunters, and members of Unitarian churches in Boston are kidnappers.

I have in my church black men, fugitive slaves. They are the crown of my apostleship, the seal of my ministry. It becomes me to look after their bodies in order to "save their souls." This law has brought us into the most intimate connection with the sin of slavery. I have been obliged to take my own parishioners into my house to keep them out of the clutches of the kidnapper. Yes, gentlemen, I have been obliged to do that; and then to keep my doors guarded by day as well as by night. Yes, I have had to arm myself. I have written my sermons with a pistol in my desk,— loaded, with a cap on the nipple, and ready for action. Yea, with a drawn sword within reach of my right hand. This I have done in Boston; in the middle of the nineteenth century; have been obliged to do it to defend the innocent members of my own church, women as well as men!

. . . A Parishioner of my brother Gannett came to kidnap a member of my church; Mr. Gannett preaches a sermon to justify the Fugitive Slave Law demanding that it should be obeyed; yes, calling on his church members to kidnap mine, and sell them into bondage forever.

Yet all this while Mr. Gannett calls himself a "Christian," and me an "infidel;" his doctrine is "Christianity," mine only "infidelity," "deism, at the best!"

O my brothers, I am not afraid of men, I can offend them. I care nothing for their hate, or their esteem. I am not very careful of my reputation. But I should not dare to violate the eternal law of God. You have called me "infidel." Surely I differ widely enough from you in my theology. But there is one thing I cannot fail to trust; that is the Infinite God, Father of the white man, Father also of the white man's slave. I should not dare violate His laws, come what may come;—should you? Nay, I can love nothing so well as I love my God.

By mid-century, Unitarianism had largely moved beyond the doctrinal battles over the Trinity and miracles, and even over Transcendentalism (which was gradually being absorbed), to the larger and deeper work of defining and perfecting American society. The creation of a distinctive American literature and history was dominated by Unitarians because in addition to training and leisure they possessed the intellectual freedom and cultural sensitivity required for the task. In the sphere of social change it was the Unitarians, affirming the moral perfectability that lies at the center of all revolution and reform, who initiated many of the great philanthropic, social, and educational reforms of the century: Joseph Tuckerman's ministry to the poor of Boston, Samuel Gridley Howe's aid to the blind, Dorothea Dix's care of the insane, Horace Mann's labors for universal, unsectarian education, and the thundering abolitionism of Parker and Garrison. These were times of high vision and strong action with Samuel Longfellow voicing the liberal Christian hope in great Unitarian hymns, Frederic Henry Hedge creating the classic translation of Martin Luther's hymn, "A Mighty Fortress is our God," James Freeman Clarke asserting the unity within diversity of world religions, and Thomas Starr King confirming California's loyalty to freedom and Union during the Civil War.

For the Unitarian denomination, the 1840's and 1850's were decades of slow church-building—with new societies formed in Toronto, Detroit, and San Francisco—and rapid progress in education—at Meadville Theological School, Meadville, Pennsylvania, established in 1844, and Antioch College, Yellow Springs, Ohio, and Washington University, St. Louis, established in 1853 (the first two founded initially by the Christian Connection). That year—1853—was also the year of the famous American Unitarian Association "creed" avowing the Executive Committee's "belief in the Divine origin, the Divine authority, the Divine sanctions of the religion of Jesus Christ" against the infidelities of Parkerism. Yet in spite of the American Unitarian Association many of the younger ministers were coming over to Parker's side, and only a faculty veto prevented him from being Divinity School commencement speaker in 1857. Not another Divinity School Address!

Amid the massive ferment of individualism, it was the Civil War which finally brought the denomination, like the Republic, to structural maturity. Henry W. Bellows, minister of All Souls Church in New York and wartime organizer of the United States Sanitary Commission, in 1864 recognized the need for a strong Unitarian organization to inspire, coordinate, and finance postwar expansion.

*In the full flush of impending Union victory he therefore spear-
headed the National Convention (later Conference) of Unitarian
Churches in New York in April 1865 "to consider the interests of
our cause and to institute measures for its good." Four hundred
delegates attended, representing almost two hundred churches. Here
are excerpts from the floor debate over the name and purposes of the
new organization, and from its Constitution.*[40]

The Rev. Dr. Bellows, from the committee of twelve, offered a
report recommending a "National Conference of Unitarian
Churches," consisting of three delegates from each church, to meet
annually. A draft of a proposed constitution and by-laws accompanied the report. The report was accepted. The question then
came up on the adoption of the constitution.

The Rev. Mr. Wasson of Cincinnati did not think this constitution would meet the wants of the times. All Christian sects accepted the Lord Jesus Christ; but the Orthodox, when they spoke
of him, meant God. While the speaker recognized the leadership
of Christ, he did not wish to use a name which had an uncertain
signification. He could not accept a Lord who was not God. The
term, Son of God should not be confined in its application to Jesus
Christ. The speaker's remarks were aimed at the expressions in the
preamble, "God and his Son" and "disciples of the Lord Jesus
Christ."

The chair ruled that this preamble would not come up for adoption until each of the articles had been disposed of.

The first article was then taken up for consideration:

C. C. Burleigh of Florence, Mass., claimed that Paul used the
expression "Mister" (translated "Master") "Jesus Christ," and not
"Lord Jesus Christ."

The Rev. Dr. Lothrop, of Boston, called the speaker to order,
inasmuch as he represented no church.

The Chair called the House to order for violating the rule in
regard to demonstrations of applause.

The Secretary stated that the credentials of Mr. Burleigh had
been received.

The Chair stated that, as the preamble was not under discussion,
the speaker's remarks were not in order.

Mr. Burleigh apologized for not having spoken to the subject, and concluded with a few general remarks.

The Rev. Dr. [James Freeman] Clarke, of Boston, moved to amend by adding after "Unitarian" the words "and Independent," so as to read "Unitarian and Independent Churches."

The Rev. Dr. Bellows thought that this was not the time to introduce that amendment, but that it would be a proper question for a future convention to consider, when the "broad church" basis would be proposed.

The Rev. Dr. Clarke consented to withdraw his amendment with some reluctance.

On motion of Mr. Elliot, speeches on the adoption of the constitution were limited to five minutes.

The Rev. Mr. Towne, of Medford, regretted the withdrawal of the amendment of Dr. Clarke. Dr. Bellows's own church was called the "First Congregational." He wanted the door opened so as to let in all, including spiritualists and come-outers. He claimed that Christ was a servant, not a Lord, and his followers should be regarded as servants. Universalists were waiting to be added to our body.

The Rev. Mr. Ames, of Albany, said that a strife about words was useless. Whatever we called ourselves, the world would call us Unitarians. He regarded this meeting as merely a squad drill. Other work was to be done hereafter, until there should be one fold and one shepherd. He did not favor letting in confessedly irreligious organizations, for the result would be the coming in of Christ with a scourge of small cords to drive everything out of the temple.

Mr. Park, of Roxbury moved to strike out "Unitarian," and insert "Free Christian."

Mr. Harlow, of Medford, seconded the amendment.

The Rev. Dr. Osgood, of New York, said that while we had affinity for other Christian bodies we came here as Unitarians. He preferred the name "Broad Church Unitarians."

Mr. Livermore, of Cambridge, regretted the motion to amend. The laymen would not consent to relinquish the name Unitarian.

The Rev. Mr. Buckingham, of Troy, had been long opposed to the use of the name Unitarian.

Mr. Mills, of Brooklyn, preferred to go with Mr. Low and have a creed, to abandoning the name Unitarian. The majority of the

Second Unitarian Society of Brooklyn were in favor of an expression of belief. He was opposed to uniting with rag, tag, and bobtail.

The Rev. Dr. Eliot moved the previous question. Ordered.

The amendment of Mr. Park was then put and lost by a decisive vote. The first article of the constitution was then adopted as reported. . . .

The preamble was then adopted by a very decisive vote.

PREAMBLE

Whereas, The great opportunities and demands for Christian labor and consecration at this time increase our sense of the obligations of all disciples of the Lord Jesus Christ to prove their faith by self-denial and by the devotion of their lives and possessions to the service of God and the building up of the Kingdom of his Son—

ARTICLE FIRST

Therefore, the Christian churches of the Unitarian faith here assembled unite themselves in a common body, to be known as the National Conference of Unitarian Churches, to the end of reorganizing and stimulating the denomination with which they are connected to the largest exertions in the cause of Christian faith and work.

ARTICLE SECOND

This National Conference shall be composed of such delegates elected annually, not to exceed three from any church, including its minister, who shall officially be one, as any of our churches may accredit to it by a certificate of their appointment.

ARTICLE THIRD

The American Unitarian Association, the Western Conference, and such other theological, academic or humane organizations in our body as the conference may see fit to invite, shall be entitled to representation by no more than three delegates each. . . .

ARTICLE SEVENTH

The National Conference, until further advised by its experience, adopts the existing organizations of the Unitarian body as the instru-

ments of its power, and confines itself to the recommending to
them such undertakings and methods as it judges to be in the heart
of the Unitarian denomination.

The achievements of the National Conference of Unitarian
Churches have been summed up in two words: organization and
orthodoxy. As a permanent association of churches, nationwide in
scope, and committed to vigorous fund-raising and expansion, it
greatly strengthened the denomination. But the Conference's "official" theology, as reflected in the Constitution, was emphatically
conservative. Unitarianism was still trying to define itself within the
Christian tradition.

A few who attended the 1865 convention, followers of Parker,
were apprehensive. Their fears were confirmed the next year in Syracuse at the first annual meeting of the National Conference, where
after heated debate the Conference reaffirmed its Christian position.
This group, notably Francis Ellingwood Abbot and William J. Potter, saw the "Battle of Syracuse" as a conflict between regimentation
and freedom. Abbot left Syracuse, as one historian has written, "convinced that Unitarianism had renounced forever its ancient principle
of free inquiry, that henceforward Christianity and freedom must
be irreconcilable foes."

The result was the formation in 1867 of the Free Religious Association, which welded the humanistic revolt against Christianity
into a single movement based on individual freedom of belief, the
scientific study of religion, and the conviction that a single, universal
spirit underlay all historic faiths. Although never large, the Free
Religious Association possessed brilliant leadership in Abbot, Potter,
O. B. Frothingham, and Felix Adler. Through tracts, lectures, and
periodicals, Free Religion made itself felt in three principal ways:
it provided a religious basis for the scientific revolt against Christianity; it pioneered in attacking denominational exclusiveness through
its emphasis on the universality of religion; and it stimulated the
transformation of Unitarianism from a Christian into a flexible and
pragmatic theism.

Abbot, the Free Religious Association's philosopher and chief
organizer, summed up the view of Free Religion as the culmination
of world history in "Fifty Affirmations" of Free Religion.[41]

FIFTY AFFIRMATIONS

"RELIGION"

(1) Religion is the effort of man to perfect himself.

(2) The root of religion is universal human nature.

(3) Historical religions are all one, in virtue of this one common root.

(4) Historical religions are all different, in virtue of their different historical origin and development.

(5) Every historical religion has thus two distinct elements,—one universal or spiritual, and the other special or historical.

(6) The universal element is the same in all historical religions; the special element is peculiar in each of them.

(7) The universal and the special elements are equally essential to the existence of an historical religion.

(8) The unity of all religions must be sought in their universal element.

(9) The peculiar character of each religion must be sought in its special element.

[Numbers 10-21 describe the "Relation of Judaism to Christianity"; 22-31 describe Christianity: "The Church of Rome embodies Christianity in its most highly developed and perfect form"; "Liberal Christianity . . . is the highest development of the free spirit of protest against authority which is possible within the Christian church."]

"FREE RELIGION"

(32) The Protestant Reformation was the birth of Free Religion, —the beginning of the religious protest against authority within the confines of the Christian Church.

(33) The history of Protestantism is the history of the growth of Free Religion at the expense of the Christian Religion. As love of freedom increases, reverence for authority decreases.

(34) The completion of the religious protest against authority must be the extinction of faith in the Christian Confession [i.e., the belief that Jesus was the Messiah].

(35) Free Religion is emancipation from the outward law, and voluntary obedience to the inward law.

(36) The great faith or moving power of Free Religion is faith in man as a progressive being.

(37) The great ideal end of Free Religion is the perfection or complete development of man,—the race serving the individual, the individual serving the race.

(38) The great practical means of Free Religion is the integral, continuous and universal education of man.

(39) The great law of Free Religion is the still, small voice of the private soul.

(40) The great peace of Free Religion is spiritual oneness with the infinite One.

(41) Free Religion is the natural outcome of every historical religion,—the final unity, therefore, towards which all historical religions slowly tend.

"RELATION OF CHRISTIANITY TO FREE RELIGION"

(42) Christianity is identical with Free Religion so far as its universal element is concerned,—antagonistic to it so far as its special element is concerned.

(43) The corner-stone of Christianity is faith in the Christ. The corner-stone of Free Religion is faith in Human Nature.

(44) The great institution of Christianity is the Christian Church, the will of Christ being its supreme law. The great institution of Free Religion is the coming Republic of the World, the universal conscience and reason of mankind being its supreme organic law or constitution.

(45) The fellowship of Christianity is limited by the Christian Confession; its brotherhood includes all subjects of the Christ and excludes all others. The fellowship of Free Religion is universal and free; it proclaims the great brotherhood of man without limit or bound.

(46) The practical work of Christianity is to Christianize the world,—to convert all souls to the Christ, and ensure their salvation from the wrath of God. The practical work of Free Religion is to humanize the world,—to make the individual nobler here and now, and to convert the human race into a vast Co-operative Union devoted to universal ends.

(47) The spiritual ideal of Christianity is the suppression of self and perfect imitation of Jesus the Christ. The spiritual ideal of

Free Religion is the free development of self, and the harmonious
education of all its powers to the highest possible degree.

(48) The essential spirit of Christianity is that of self-humiliation
at the feet of Jesus, and passionate devotion to his person. The essential spirit of Free Religion is that of self-respect and free self-
devotion to great ideas. Christianity is prostrate on its face; Free
Religion is erect on its feet.

(49) The noblest fruit of Christianity is a self-sacrificing love of
man for Jesus' sake.—The noblest fruit of Free Religion is a self-
sacrificing love of man for man's own sake.

(50) Christianity is the faith of the soul's childhood; Free Religion is the faith of the soul's manhood. In the gradual growth of
mankind out of Christianity into Free Religion, lies the only hope
of the spiritual perfection of the individual and the spiritual unity of
the race.

*Free Religion was the come-outism of American Unitarianism.
Its adherents were sure of what they did not want in religion, but
found it almost impossible to agree on what they did want. The
Free Religious Association declined from inaction, and finally dis-
integrated from the centrifugal forces of radical individualism. Its
work culminated and for all practical purposes ended with the World
Parliament of Religions in Chicago in 1893.*

*Perhaps the main sectional stronghold of Free Religion was the
Western Unitarian Conference, formed in 1852 to advance the work
of Unitarian churches west of New York State. The Western
churches were in the same position vis-à-vis New England Unitarianism as were the Episcopal churches of colonial New England vis-à-
vis the Church of England—separated by a gulf of distance and
ideas which made ecclesiastical control extremely difficult. Differences between the freedom-minded Western churches and the more
conservative Eastern leaders of the denomination reached a crisis
in 1875. The Western Conference withdrew its support from the
American Unitarian Association's missionary program and hired its
own Missionary Secretary, the Rev. Jenkin Lloyd Jones. Jones became for a decade the "St. Paul" of Western Unitarianism, organizing churches from the Appalachians to the Rockies, all in the name
of "Freedom, Fellowship, and Character in Religion," the Conference's motto. To a substantial group of Westerners, however, Jones'*

rallying cry sounded suspiciously like that of the Free Religious Association—"Freedom and Fellowship." This group, headed by the Rev. Jabez T. Sunderland of Ann Arbor and the Rev. Jasper Douthit of Shelbyville, Illinois, would have preferred to see Jones organizing new churches in the name of Jesus Christ.

Thus in the 1880's arose "The Issue in the West," to which Sunderland, now Jones' successor as Missionary Secretary, gave classic expression in a pamphlet written for the Western Conference annual meeting in 1886.[42]

Is Western Unitarianism Ready to Give Up Its Christian Character?

Is it Ready to Give Up Its Theistic Character?

. . . Plainly, Western Unitarianism has reached a question which it must face. That question is no other than the one (one question in two forms) which has been placed at the head of this paper. Are we ready to declare that those great faiths—in God, prayer, immortality and the spiritual leadership of Jesus—which have always in the past been at the very heart of Unitarianism, are no longer essential to our movement?

Unitarianism in the past has always been Christian. Nobody thinks of doubting that. Our great historic leaders, the men who have given luster to the Unitarian name—Channing, the Wares, Parker, [Orville] Dewey, Bellows, to say nothing of those now living—have all stood for Liberal Christianity. Unitarianism in England, Europe, and all foreign lands where it is known does the same today. So does it in New England and the Middle States and the South and on the Pacific Coast. So has it always in the West, without dispute and without a question, until within a very few years. So does it indeed, doubtless, with a great majority of the Unitarians of the West still. But, within a dozen years or so, seemingly as the result of the breaking over the West of the free religious wave of the East, there has been a movement here, at first quite unnoticed, possibly hardly conscious of itself, but becoming more definite in its purpose and more pronounced as it went on, to create a new and different order of Unitarianism in the West. From the beginning, this new Unitarianism has shown an especially warm sympathy with the Free Religious movement, and later, with the Ethical movement; has steadily sought to differentiate itself from the Unitarianism of the East as being something "broader" and "more advanced" than that, has long been averse to the use of the Christian name, and for a few years past has been more and more distinctly moving off from even a theistic basis, until now it declares openly and strongly that even belief in God must no longer be declared an essential of Unitarianism.

To avoid misunderstanding, it should be said at the outset, however, that most of the men who are thus endeavoring to remove the Unitarianism of the West onto this new basis, are themselves, personally, believers in God, prayer and immortality,—as they are unquestionably sincere in their expressed wish that all individual Unitarians might be believers in the same. But, they say, all this must be left solely to the individual. Unitarian churches as churches, Unitarian organizations as organizations, the Unitarian denomination as a denomination, must not plant themselves upon these beliefs. Unitarianism must stand for ethical beliefs and beliefs in certain so-called "principles," but not for belief in anything that will commit it to theism or Christianity. The particular beliefs which are most often and most strongly insisted upon by this new school are four, viz.: Belief in "freedom," belief in "fellowship," belief in "character," and, by implication, belief in "religion." . . .

I need hardly say that for a number of years past warning voices have not been few in the West, telling of trouble certainly ahead if the attempt was persisted in of thus revolutionizing Western Unitarianism. Mr. Douthit after several years of protest inside the Western Conference withdrew from that body because of its extreme non-Christian tendencies. . . . The warnings of Dr. [William Greenleaf] Eliot, of St. Louis, have been frequent and very earnest. The Meadville men have been greatly troubled at the tendency of things. . . .

It would seem that all these protests and warnings surely ought to have caused our "freedom, fellowship and character" friends to reflect how revolutionary a thing they were undertaking, and how certainly, if persevered in, it must bring discord and division all over the West, where there used to be, and ought to be still, union, harmony and peace. And if there are any voices of controversy beginning to be heard in any quarter among us to-day, or if anywhere

the harmony and unity of spirit among churches and ministers is
less than we could desire, can any one mistake as to where the responsibility rests? Surely it can rest only in one place, and that is
with the innovators. Surely it can lie at only one door, and that is
the door of that party of good and loved but singularly misjudging
men who have disturbed the historic order, and undertaken the
task of removing the body to a new basis,—a new basis so ultra, so
unprecedented in its character, and, at least to many minds, so
essentially unreasonable, that a moment's reflection ought to have
made it plain that the denomination in the West could never accept it. . . .

The issue before the West is not one of creed or no creed. Nobody wants a creed; nobody, so far as I am aware, would have a
creed if he could. . . . But this cannot justly be made to imply
that we have not stood or do not stand for any doctrinal belief, as
a denomination. It only means that we have not been willing to
make formulated and authorized and not-to-be-changed definitions
and statements of our belief. We have always stood, and it is a
very new and strange condition of things if we do not still stand,
in a large way, in a fluent, elastic way, in an undogmatic and non-
credal way, . . . for the great, simple, primal, self-evidencing faiths
of religion—God, worship, the immortal life, the supremacy of character, the spiritual leadership of Jesus.

. . . Mr. [William Channing] Gannett tells us that the denomination first took its stand on "reason and revelation," but it had to
move on. Later it took its stand at the supernatural or the miraculous; but it had to move on. Later still it made another stand at the
Lordship of Christ, but again it was compelled to move on. Now the
stand is made at Christian theism, but once more, he says, we must
move on. Move on where? . . .

The fact seems to be, there is nothing about which there is more
mental confusion than about this whole moving on idea. . . . If I
am faced toward the edge of Table rock, Niagara, I can safely move
on for a distance—move on until I am within 20 feet of the edge,
15 feet, 10 feet, 5 feet, 2 feet, one foot—but if I move on much
beyond that it will be the last moving on I shall be likely to do in
this world. So a religious body may move on for a time toward the
edge of religion—nearer and nearer to the edge—but what if it

moves off? Our *Unity* friends have got us to the place where they
want us as a body to move on and move off historic Unitarianism—
move off Christianity, move off theism; they tell us if we will we
shall find a religion of ethics which will be better. . . .

. . . As to the future,. the signs of promise that I see on every
hand are simply magnificent, if we are firm and clear-visioned, and
go forward with bravery and faith, with one hand holding with
absolute fidelity to our priceless Christian heritages from the past,
and with the other reaching out with absolute confidence to grasp
God's not less precious gifts and revelations of the present. But
failing of this—turning aside from the great highway so plainly before us, into any such by-path meadow as our loved and honored
and certainly well-meaning but as certainly mistaken *Unity* brethren
urge—I can see nothing before us but a future of sad disappointments
and regrets. By hauling.down and destroying our theistic and Christian flags and running up in their place the ethical only, I am convinced we should seal the fate of Unitarianism as a religious movement in the West. . . .

*The controversy between the Western Christians and the liberals
(also called the "Unity men" because their leader, Jones, edited the
Conference weekly by that name) raged hard and loud. Sunderland
and Douthit formed a rival Western Unitarian Association among
the theistic churches. In Boston the directors of the American Unitarian Association avowed that they "would regard it as a subversion
of the purpose for which its funds have been contributed . . . to
give assistance to any church or organization which does not rest
emphatically on the Christian basis."*

*At the next meeting of the Western Unitarian Conference in
Chicago in 1887, the Rev. William Channing Gannett proposed a
doctrinal compromise in a statement entitled "Things Commonly
Believed Among Us." He introduced it on the condition that it
was not binding on "a single member . . . , the statement being
always open to re-statement and to be regarded only as the thought
of the majority." Gannett had struck to the root of the controversy:
neither side felt secure in its freedom. The Christians feared a conspiracy to deprive them of God and Jesus; the liberals feared every
move that suggested uniformity of belief. Remove the threat of*

deprivation and coercion and where was the disagreement? "The difference is the smallest that ever kept men apart who belong together," said one minister afterward.

"Things Commonly Believed Among Us" was adopted, 59 to 13. It paved the way for an eventual reconciliation in the Western Conference in 1894, and represents Western Unitarianism at its best.[43]

The Western Conference has neither the wish nor the right to bind a single member by declarations concerning fellowship or doctrine. Yet it thinks some practical good may be done by setting forth in simple words the things most commonly believed among us,—the Statement being always open to re-statement and to be regarded only as the thought of the majority.

All names that divide "religion" are to us of little consequence compared with religion itself. Whoever loves Truth and lives the Good is, in a broad sense, of our religious fellowship; whoever loves the one or lives the other better than ourselves is our teacher, whatever church or age he may belong to.

The general faith is hinted well in words which several of our churches have adopted for their covenant: "In the freedom of the Truth and in the spirit of Jesus Christ, we unite for the worship of God and the service of man." It is hinted in such words as these: "Unitarianism is a religion of love to God and love to man." Because we have no "creed" which we impose as a condition of fellowship, specific statements of belief abound among us, always somewhat differing, always largely agreeing. One such we offer here:

"We believe that to love the Good and to live the Good is the supreme thing in religion;

"We hold reason and conscience to be final authorities in matters of religious belief;

"We honor the Bible and all inspiring scripture, old and new;

"We revere Jesus, and all holy souls that have taught men truth and righteousness and love, as prophets of religion.

"We believe in the growing nobility of Man;

"We trust the unfolding Universe as beautiful, beneficent, unchanging Order; to know this order is truth; to obey it is right and liberty and stronger life;

"We believe that good and evil invariably carry their own recompense, no good thing being failure and no evil thing success; that heaven and hell are states of being; that no evil can befall the good man in either life or death; that all things work together for the victory of Good.

"We believe that we ought to join hands and work to make the good things better and the worst good, counting nothing good for self that is not good for all;

"We believe that this self-forgetting, loyal life awakes in man the sense of union here and now with things eternal—the sense of deathlessness; and this sense is to us an earnest of the life to come.

"We worship One-in-All—that life whence suns and stars derive their orbits and the soul of man its Ought,—that Light which lighteth every man that cometh into the world, giving us power to become the sons of God,—that Love with which our souls commune."

The Twentieth Century: Humanism and Theism
in a New Age

Unitarianism during the nineteenth century became an "accept-able" religion. It was different, to be sure, from other religions, but the differences were nothing heretical. Thus the turn of the twen-tieth century found Unitarianism in a contented slumber. Having moved beyond Channing it hadn't yet caught up with Parker, but it didn't know it. The world was satisfactory just as it was.

The liberal movement did not really enter the twentieth century until 1914. The World War shattered the foundations of nineteenth-century society—custom, order, self-reliance—and with them the foundations of nineteenth-century liberalism. As the ultimate themes of freedom and tragedy, greed and death flamed anew, the former assurance of "the progress of mankind onward and upward forever" seemed no longer to be warranted by the facts. Nevertheless the liberals were hopeful, trusting in good will, education, and science to usher in the Kingdom of God in a reasonable time.

Now at mid-century the Kingdom of God is increasingly acknowl-edged to be unattainable in human society. The Kingdom of God is not a social structure but a spirit within, which enhances and transforms social structures in humanity's quest for truth and justice and fulfillment. In the light of this conception there is growing evi-dence that the church of Servetus and Parker may yet speak for God to the Hydrogen Age.

The Unitarian years after 1887 were relatively peaceful. Many of the leaders of earlier controversies gave up their places to young men with new goals. Several outstanding ministries began during the period, including those of Samuel A. Eliot, Earl Morse Wilbur, and John Haynes Holmes. Interest in world Unitarianism culmi-nated in the formation in 1900 of the International Association for Liberal Christianity and Religious Freedom. In 1909 President Charles W. Eliot of Harvard predicted that "the religion of the future" would "not deal chiefly with sorrow and death, but with joy and life." It would, he said, have as its chief precept "Be serviceable" and would harmonize with the "great secular movements of modern society." Other liberals of the period, among them Professor Francis Greenwood Peabody of the Harvard Divinity School, were aware of the work of certain scholars who called into question the idea of ethical progress and pointed to the radical eschatology of the New Testament; one of these was Albert Schweitzer in his The Quest of the Historical Jesus (1906). Nevertheless the denominational mood in the years after 1887, in contrast with the previous and pending decades, was one of relative theological peacefulness.

The "peacefulness" of the period ended with the advent of religious humanism, the most significant theological development of the new century. Catching up the scientific and anti-supernaturalist currents of the day, humanism voiced them as a new world religion for a new day. Its first advocates were the Rev. John H. Dietrich in Spokane, Washington, who joined the Unitarians after the Reformed church had expelled him for heresy, and the Rev. Curtis W. Reese in Des Moines, Iowa, a former Baptist. Another pioneer humanist was Dr. Charles Francis Potter, who later founded the First Humanist Society of New York.

Dietrich and Reese began preaching humanism in 1913. Their message of humanity's uniqueness in an indifferent universe was enthusiastically received in the Midwest, as Free Religion and Ethical Unitarianism had been received before it. But when the rumblings of humanism penetrated the slower-moving East, a generation-long "humanist-theist controversy" broke out in earnest. A major stimulus to the controversy was an address by Reese at the Harvard Summer School of Theology in 1920, entitled "The Content of Present-Day Religious Liberalism." [44]

Historically the basic content of religious liberalism is spiritual freedom. Out of this basic content has come the conviction of the supremacy of reason, of the primary worth of character, and of the immediate access of man to spiritual sources. Always religious liberalism has tended to replace alleged divine revelations and commands with human opinions and judgments; to develop the individual attitude in religion; and to identify righteousness with life. The method of religious liberalism has always been that of reflection, not that of authority. Liberalism has insisted on the essentially natural character of religion.

Believing that religion is best promoted in the presence of live issues, and that every age must achieve its own faith, liberalism has been willing to hazard its affirmations in an open field where the contestants strive for only the greatest service possible. And this experience has led liberalism not only to free religion from extraneous accretions, but also to think of religion primarily as conscious committal and loyalty to human causes and goals. Formerly liberalism emphasized chiefly emancipation and freedom; now it emphasizes also committal and loyalty.

Liberalism has had to face, even more than have other forms of religion, the age-old philosophical question "why?" That is, to what purpose—to what end—do we live? In answer to this question humanistic liberalism proclaims as the end and aim of religion, and of life, free and positive personality, loyally and intelligently associated, and cosmically related.

If liberalism can be reduced to a single statement, I think this is it: Conscious committal and loyalty to worthful causes and goals in order that free and positive personality may be developed, intelligently associated, and cosmically related.

Let us see where this leads.

The liberal is not satisfied with a religious experience acquired chiefly through confession, repentance and divine communion, and terminating in a heaven of subject existence. He is not willing to accept the promise of a distant estate of doubtful character and location in lieu of concrete worths and measurable values here and now. He believes that whatever the future may hold for him it must be the outcome of his own spiritual achievements. Hence he demands that his personality be free and self-directive.

The liberal is not satisfied with purely material ends. In his swing away from mystic union with entities of doubtful existence he does not plunge into the abyss of gross material satisfactions. He may go from one of these extremes to the other, but if so, it is only for a while. In the long run he hangs tenaciously to the conviction that fundamentally his nature is spiritual—that a spiritual self adjusts and guides and controls.

The liberal is not satisfied with freedom alone. Emancipated from superstition and prejudice, he may lead a care-free and easy existence for a while, but soon the essentially positive nature of personality becomes assertive, and the liberal knows that positive committals and loyalty are essential to the full expression of himself.

The center of spiritual gravity is shifted from objective and supernatural forms to individual man. This is not the denial of the existence of significant and objective worths, but only the removal of the seat of authority from an indefinite something somewhere, to a definite self known to be native to human existence. This is not a hasty conclusion reached by the liberal. It is the plainly observable trend of history. The lesson of the long experience of the race is that of the primary importance of human initiative and self-direction.

The outstanding characteristic of modern liberalism, and indeed of all modern thinking, is the evaluation of personality as the thing of supreme worth. Hence liberalism now affirms in terms unmistakable that institutions are only the tentative and temporary expressions of personality, that they are frequently outgrown and must, like the hull of the chrysalis, be burst asunder and left only to mark an epoch past. Institutions—religious, capitalistic, socialistic, or what not—must now stand or fall as they are able or unable to serve effectively and efficiently in the building of free and positive human souls.

Present-day liberals see the essentially interdependent nature of human beings; that the fulfillment of the individual self requires orderly, purposeful association with other selves. This thought finds expression in various terms: Brotherhood, solidarity, mutuality, reciprocity, fraternity, community. For a long time prophets, poets and statesmen have proclaimed the ambition of the race to be linked together for mutual service; and now biology and social science agree that there is and can be no complete self-realization aside from co-operation with other selves.

Ideally this is the heart of Christianity. The organic unity of the race is found in the teachings of Christianity. Jesus, at his best, thought and spoke in world-terms. Human solidarity is the heart of the labor movement. This finds expression in the motto: "An injury to one is an injury to all." The red flag is meant to be symbolic of the blood of the race. The latest and best type of statesmanship thinks in world terms. We are now becoming accustomed to world issues, programs and achievements.

Humanistic liberalism constantly aims to promote the widest possible human comradeship and the closest possible human fellowship. And this aim is underwritten by the knowledge that co-operation and not competition is the dominant factor in the growth of the race.

In the most intimate of human relationships, the home, we know no complete satisfaction apart from the good of those whom we love. Notions of the exact character of this relationship, laws defining its social responsibilities may and do and should change with changing time; but always the race finds deep and abiding satisfaction in the solidarity of what we call home. We now know that the positive sentiments and other hard facts of the solidarity of the home belong essentially to other social relationships. In industry we are trying as never before, and with a measure of success, to reorganize on the basis of community interests. So with other relationshps. The old notion that the individual experiencing good can be an isolated individual has gone forever.

The legacy from the best prophets of the past is a conception of a united world. The coming order is a world order. And any religion that hesitates to proclaim this gospel is neither an heir of the prophets of the past nor the parent of the achievement of the future.

The cohesive principle in the achievement of this human world order is radical good-will. This leads to the new competition, competition in the rendering of the greatest service. The pride of the old professions—law, medicine, ministry—is in the rendering of the greatest service. The spirit of the old professions must be fused into the social order from bottom to top, from the corner grocery to the League of Nations.

Liberals think of Democracy not only as freedom and equality of opportunity but also as mutual assistance in the use of freedom and opportunity. To take one class off the shoulder of another class is not enough. All people must work shoulder to shoulder.

Radical good-will alone does not satisfy humanistic liberalism. Now comes the demand on good-will to develop a technique for making itself effective in the world of hard facts. Social science is still in its infancy. There is room for and need of creative statesmanship in the reorganization of human relationships. How to secure food, shelter, and clothes without losing one's soul is a pressing problem. At last humanity has rebelled against a state of affairs that requires the forfeiture of the soul in order to acquire a rag, a shack, and a loaf of bread. In the solution of the problems involved in the rescue of the soul from the clutch of mammon are causes worthy of committal and loyalty. Liberalism declares that the church needs to understand the economic expression of brotherhood, and that everybody needs to understand the spiritual significance of economic co-operation. The next step in world progress is the proper co-ordination of economic forces with intellectual, moral, and spiritual forces.

In the past the basic content of most religions has been that of the submission of persons to supernatural agencies, and the consequent appropriation of worths. In these systems of religion man was worthful because he participated in or was possessed by supernatural agencies. In virtue of this relation man received a supply of finished goods. In these systems men got their rights, powers, and goods by servile tenure. There was submission from below and control from above. This monarchic view of religion rose to its noblest height in the expression, "Thy will be done."

The realm of the divine is now subject to investigation. Here, as elsewhere, the scientific method is being applied. Here regulated observation and experiment may result in new theological discoveries, and so liberalism must remain undogmatic in regard to God. The theology of Augustine and that of Channing, the theology of Billy Sunday and that of H. G. Wells, might all be found utterly inadequate without consequent injury to the religion of the liberal. Liberalism is building a religion that would not be shaken even if the thought of God were out-grown.

Nevertheless, the liberal recognizes and zealously proclaims the fact that purposive and powerful cosmic processes are operative, and that increasingly man is able to co-operate with them and in a measure control them. What these processes be styled is of but little importance. Some call them cosmic processes, others call them God. In life there is wisdom beyond our present comprehension. This is seen in the amoeba as it adjusts its structure for the attainment of the ends desired; in the living protoplasmic cells on the ends of the rootlets of bean and wheat, both apparently identical, the one refusing flint, the other receiving it; in the co-operative colony of the sponge and the daisy, the bee and the wolf; and in the marvellous neural arrangement of man.

To the ancients the contemplation of cosmic events led to the theory of direct supernatural operation or to that of the use of natural forces by supernatural agencies. But to an increasing number of serious thinkers and to an innumerable host of liberals everywhere the contemplation of cosmic events has given way to regulated observation of and experiment with cosmic purposes; and this has led to conscious co-operation with and partial control of cosmic processes. The ancients bowed before the unknown; the modern man attempts to understand the unknown. Supernatural agencies and laws are giving way to natural modes and processes. With this must go much of the nomenclature and many of the forms of worship of the religions of the world.

Humanistic liberalism understands spirituality to be man at his best, sane in mind, healthy in body, dynamic in personality; honestly facing the hardest facts, conquering and not fleeing from his gravest troubles; committed to the most worthful causes, loyal to the best ideals; ever hoping, striving, and achieving. To know one's self as inherently worthful, actually to find fullest expression in the widest human service and consciously to become a co-worker with cosmic processes, is spiritual experience deep and abiding.

According to Reese, "There was much excitement in the discussion from the floor that immediately followed the address. One minister cried to high Heaven that he would rather have his right arm severed from his body than to take God away from the people."

In the ensuing controversy the Rev. John Dietrich's debates with the Rev. W. L. Sullivan and his preaching in the Unitarian church in Minneapolis (where he had moved in 1916) won for humanism many friends—and enemies. The Scopes trial in 1926 dramatized the issue of naturalism vs. supernaturalism for the world to judge. Throughout the decade increasing numbers of Unitarians and Unitarian churches joined the humanist ranks.

In the Winter of 1932-1933 a group of Chicago humanists attempted to state humanism's basic affirmations in "A Humanist Manifesto." The first draft was written by Professor Roy Wood Sellars of the University of Michigan and amended in consultation *with the eventual signers and many others who decided not to sign. Here is the "Humanist Manifesto" complete.[45]*

The time has come for widespread recognition of the radical changes in religious beliefs throughout the modern world. The time is past for mere revision of traditional attitudes. Science and economic change have disrupted the old beliefs. Religions the world over are under the necessity of coming to terms with new conditions created by a vastly increased knowledge and experience. In every field of human activity, the vital movement is now in the direction of a candid and explicit humanism. In order that religious humanism may be better understood we, the undersigned, desire to make certain affirmations which we believe the facts of our contemporary life demonstrate.

There is great danger of a final, and we believe fatal, identification of the word "religion" with doctrines and methods which have lost their significance and which are powerless to solve the problems of human living in the Twentieth Century. Religions have always been means for realizing the highest values of life. Their end has been accomplished through the interpretation of the total environing situation (theology or world view), the sense of values resulting therefrom (goal or ideal), and the technique (cult), established for realizing a satisfactory life. A change in any of these factors results in alteration of the outward forms of religion. This fact explains the changefulness of religions through the centuries. But through all changes religion itself remains constant in its quest for abiding values, an inseparable feature of human life.

Today man's larger understanding of the universe, his scientific achievements, and his deeper appreciation of brotherhood, have created a situation which requires a new statement of the means and purposes of religion. Such a vital, fearless, and frank religion capable of furnishing adequate social goals and personal satisfactions may appear to many people as a complete break with the past. While this age does owe a vast debt to the traditional religions, it is none the less obvious that any religion that can hope to be a synthesizing and dynamic force for today must be shaped for the needs of this age. To establish such a religion is a major necessity of the present. It is a responsibility which rests upon this generation. We therefore affirm the following:

First: Religious humanists regard the universe as self-existing and not created.

Second: Humanism believes that man is a part of nature and that he has emerged as the result of a continuous process.

Third: Holding an organic view of life, humanists find that the traditional dualism of mind and body must be rejected.

Fourth: Humanism recognizes that man's religious culture and civilization, as clearly depicted by anthropology and history, are the product of a gradual development due to his interaction with his natural environment and with his social heritage. The individual born into a particular culture is largely molded by that culture.

Fifth: Humanism asserts that the nature of the universe depicted by modern science makes unacceptable any supernatural or cosmic guarantees of human values. Obviously humanism does not deny the possibility of realities as yet undiscovered, but it does insist that the way to determine the existence and value of any and all realities is by means of intelligent inquiry and by the assessment of their relations to human needs. Religion must formulate its hopes and plans in the light of the scientific spirit and method.

Sixth: We are convinced that the time has passed for theism, deism, modernism, and the several varieties of "new thought."

Seventh: Religion consists of those actions, purposes, and experiences which are humanly significant. Nothing human is alien to the religious. It includes labor, art, science, philosophy, love, friendship, recreation—all that is in its degree expressive of intelligently satisfying human living. The distinction between the sacred and the secular can no longer be maintained.

Eighth: Religious Humanism considers the complete realization of human personality to be the end of man's life and seeks its development and fulfillment in the here and now. This is the explanation of the humanist's social passion.

Ninth: In the place of the old attitudes involved in worship and prayer the humanist finds his religious emotions expressed in a heightened sense of personal life and in a co-operative effort to promote social well-being.

Tenth: It follows that there will be no uniquely religious emotions and attitudes of the kind hitherto associated with belief in the supernatural.

Eleventh: Man will learn to face the crises of life in terms of his knowledge of their naturalness and probability. Reasonable and manly attitudes will be fostered by education and supported by custom. We assume that humanism will take the path of social and mental hygiene and discourage sentimental and unreal hopes and wishful thinking.

Twelfth: Believing that religion must work increasingly for joy in living, religious humanists aim to foster the creative in man and to encourage achievements that add to the satisfactions of life.

Thirteenth: Religious humanism maintains that all associations and institutions exist for the fulfillment of human life. The intelligent evaluation, transformation, control and direction of such associations and institutions with a view to the enhancement of human life is the purpose and program of humanism. Certainly religious institutions, their ritualistic forms, ecclesiastical methods, and communal activities must be reconstituted as rapidly as experience allows, in order to function effectively in the modern world.

Fourteenth: The humanists are firmly convinced that existing acquisitive and profit-motivated society has shown itself to be inadequate and that a radical change in methods, controls, and motives must be instituted. A socialized and co-operative economic order must be established to the end that the equitable distribution of the means of life be possible. The goal of humanism is a free and universal society in which people voluntarily and intelligently co-operate for the common good. Humanists demand a shared life in a shared world.

Fifteenth and last: We assert that humanism will: (a) affirm life rather than deny it; (b) seek to elicit the possibilities of life, not flee from it; and (c) endeavor to establish the conditions of a satisfactory life for all, not merely for a few. By this positive morale and intention humanism will be guided, and from this perspective and alignment the techniques and efforts of humanism will flow.

So stand the theses of religious humanism. Though we consider the religious forms and ideas of our fathers no longer adequate, the quest for the good life is still the central task for mankind. Man is at last becoming aware that he alone is responsible for the realization of the world of his dreams, that he has within himself the power for its achievement. He must set intelligence and will to the task.

(Signed) J. A. C. Fagginger Auer, E. Burdette Backus, Harry Elmer Barnes, L. M. Birkhead, Raymond B. Bragg, Edwin Arthur

Burtt, Ernest Caldecott, A. J. Carlson, John Dewey, Albert C. Dief-
fenbach, John H. Dietrich, Bernard Fantus, William Floyd, F. H.
Hankins, A. Eustace Haydon, Llewellyn Jones, Robert Morss Lovett,
Harold P. Marley, R. Lester Mondale, Charles Francis Potter, John
Herman Randall, Jr., Curtis W. Reese, Oliver L. Reiser, Roy Wood
Sellars, Clinton Lee Scott, Maynard Shipley, W. Frank Swift, V. T.
Thayer, Eldred C. Vanderlaan, Joseph Walker, Jacob J. Weinstein,
Frank S. C. Wicks, David Rhys Williams, Edwin H. Wilson.

Note [appended to Manifesto]: The Manifesto is a product of many
minds. It was designed to represent a developing point of view, not a
new creed. The individuals whose signatures appear, would, had they
been writing individual statements, have stated the propositions in
differing terms. The importance of the document is that more than
thirty men have come to general agreement on matters of final concern and that these men are undoubtedly representative of a large
number who are forging a new philosophy out of the materials of
the modern world. It is obvous that many others might have been
asked to sign the Manifesto had not the lack of time and the short-
age of clerical assistance limited our ability to communicate with
them.

For many, the humanist-theist controversy consisted of an argument of "God-or-no-God." To the humanists it was more truly a
debate over the evidences and merit of the natural vs. supernatural
interpretations of reality. At any rate it was evidence of important
theological activity within the denomination.
Less impressive were the gains of the churches themselves. An
alarming number of Unitarian congregations, including many receiving American Unitarian Association assistance, had failed during
the first third of the century. There was a widespread feeling that
the denomination had lost its sense of purpose and that a recovery
program was needed. To this end an eight-member Commission of
Appraisal was appointed by the American Unitarian Association at
its annual meeting in 1934. The Commission's assignment was "to
survey our work both in theory and practice, to appraise the methods
now in use, and to recommend clarification of principles and changes
in policy, program, and organization." The Rev. Frederick May
Eliot, minister of Unity Church in St. Paul, Minnesota, was named

its chair. Here is an excerpt from the Commission's report, entitled
Unitarians Face a New Age.[46]

The first question which the members of the Commission of Appraisal decided must be answered, if their enquiry was to have practical value, was whether the organized religious movement known as Unitarianism has any real function to perform in the modern world. If not, it would clearly be better to liquidate the present organizations and resources, for the mere continuation of any institution after it has ceased to meet a real need is wasteful, and for this to happen to an institution calling itself "liberal" would be a tragic irony of fate.

If this question is to be answered in the affirmative, it must be in different terms from those in which the function of Unitarianism was defined a hundred years ago—or fifty, or even twenty-five. The radical spirit of the founders and re-founders of Unitarianism may be the inspiration for our present effort to re-think and re-formulate the purposes of our movement; but some of the basic ideas and certainly the specific phrases used must be worked out in the light of the present situation and under the impact of forces in the modern world impinging upon all churches. What Channing, Emerson, Parker, Henry W. Bellows, and Thomas Starr King did for their generations must be done anew for ours, but their formulas will not serve to meet our needs.

The genius of the Unitarian movement has been its power to adapt the vocabulary and practices of a religion whose roots are sunk deep into the past to new knowledge, new conditions, and new situations. If this genius should fail us now, the time will have come to write "finis" to the story of Unitarianism.

Whatever may be the actual future of the name Unitarian, there can be little doubt of the need in the modern world for some organized expression of the liberal spirit in religion. In a time when revolution and chaos are everywhere threatening, when ideals are again forming an alliance with tyranny and dogmatism, when intellectual confusion and social discontent are blindly trying to fight their way out of situations where only the problem-solving temper of mind can be of real help, when a fresh birth of the nationalistic spirit is everywhere offering its spurious comfort to tired and discouraged people—in a time like ours there is imperative need for a religious fellowship that will bring order and hope and confidence to men of the liberal tradition. . . .

What is needed in the world of 1936 is an association of free churches that will stand and fight for the central philosophy and values of liberal religion. . . . Liberal religion must express itself through liberal churches. . . . What sort of churches will these be . . . ?

To begin with, they will be churches—that is, they will be institutions made up of human beings organized to promote the development of spiritual insight and power among their own members and in society. . . . However important the adjective "liberal" may be, it will always be recognized as modifying the noun "churches." But these churches will have also certain distinguishing marks, differentiating them from the main body of churches and justifying the use of the adjective.

In the first place, they will be thoroughly emancipated from the sectarian spirit, from the tendency to set themselves up as small, select, superior groups of men and women to whom by some mysterious dispensation an exclusive gift of truth has been granted. They will cultivate an intensive sense of fellowship within their own ranks, but they will be keenly aware of the world-wide aspects of their liberal faith, recognizing the kinship of liberals across all barriers of race or nationality or traditional religious background. . . . They will not desire to "Christianize the world," because they believe that religion is deeper and more significant than any of its historic forms —even the Christian. . . .

In the second place, they will be thoroughly committed to the practice of democracy within their own organized life. Within their own area, they will serve as laboratories where new techniques of a growing democratic process may be developed and tested, for a liberal church can use the processes of democratic cooperative activity more fully than is possible in almost any other organization. They will be constantly on the alert to detect any encroachment of autocratic control within themselves or among their several units. Their only methods for securing unanimity of opinion will be persuasion and leadership; and they will be jealous in their determination to safeguard the full rights of minorities within their own ranks. . . .

In the third place, they will be characterized by a fresh discovery of the importance of leadership. There will be no priestly class within such churches and no monopoly of leadership in any special group. . . .

In the fourth place, through the development of group-thinking and group-activity in their full democratic forms, there will gradually emerge a body of common opinion which will, at any one particular time, be recognized as the common possession of the whole group. Avoiding with the utmost care any suggestion of an official creed, and insisting at every point upon the right of minorities, majorities, and the total group, to change their minds as knowledge advances, they will nevertheless be unafraid to say with some real degree of definiteness, "These are things which today we believe to be true". . . .

In the fifth place, these liberal churches will recognize the central importance of worship. . . . In this, they will recognize the psychological value of regularity and form, of the use of traditional ceremonies, symbols, and practices, and of ordered self-expression through familiar and beloved channels, both in groups and in solitude. At the same time they will . . . be alert to develop and test new ways of worship, organically related to the traditional, that shall be truly consistent with the sincerity and power of their growing religious convictions. . . .

In the sixth place, liberal churches will accept the educational method as their primary instrument for the fostering of religion and for the application of religion to human situations and problems. . . . The idea that education is only for children and adolescents will be abandoned by the churches, as it has been by everyone else. . . . They will reject the narrow interpretation of "religious education" as a sort of appendage or decoration or luxury, and will insist that the entire church program shall be redefined in terms of education, from the religious point of view and with the religious motive animating it throughout. . . .

Finally, these churches will affirm their belief that religion is futile and sterile unless it has direct and effective bearing upon the problems of human society. They will be unsparing in their criticism of the evils and injustices now existing in the world, and they will work unceasingly for a better social order. . . .

The Commission of Appraisal introduced sweeping structural changes designed to unify and revitalize the denomination. Among these were the absorption of the General Conference (formerly the National Conference of Unitarian Churches) into the American Unitarian Association thus creating a single denominational agency; the centralization of executive authority in the President; the geographic decentralization of administrative responsibility; consolidated financial planning; and the creation of a continuing Commission on Planning and Review to survey and coordinate the work of all Unitarian organizations. In addition it suggested new directions for Unitarian extension efforts, ministerial relations, theological education, and values and doctrine. At a climactic annual meeting in 1937, the American Unitarian Association accepted most of the Commission's recommendations and elected the Commission chairperson, Dr. Eliot, as its new president.

In the years since 1937 the denomination has not only recovered its direction but has pioneered. A new experience-centered approach to religious education, developed under the leadership of Sophia Lyon Fahs, has exerted a profound influence on a generation of children trained in Unitarian' (and non-Unitarian) church schools. The Unitarian Service Committee, established in 1940 to render unsectarian relief to the world's needy, has become a unique and trusted instrument of humanitarian service. A "functional" approach to church organization, whereby the structure and program of the local church is dynamically related to personal and community needs, has developed simultaneously in Toronto, St. Paul, San Diego, and other cities, and is spreading. Beginning in 1953 the consolidation of Unitarian and Universalist energies in the Council of Liberal Churches has fulfilled a century-long dream of practical cooperation and mutual aid among the liberal churches of America.

The most spectacular manifestation of denominational outreach at mid-twentieth century is the Unitarian fellowship program, an idea which—because of its inherent brilliance and ideal timing—developed into a movement in less than a decade at the close of World War Two. Although the present movement dates from 1945, today's fellowships are not the first such groups in the history of American Unitarianism. In the 1880's lay units called Sunday Circles—"little churches cradled in a home parlor"—sprouted in the Western Unitarian Conference, notably in Iowa and Illinois. A quarter-century later, in 1907, the

American Unitarian Association instituted a program of lay centers
in cities where there were no Unitarian churches. Units in Rockville,
Connecticut; Davenport, Iowa; Memphis, Tennessee, affiliated with
the Association at that time.

The present program had its formal beginnings in a resolution of
the American Unitarian Association Board of Directors in March
1945, based on a recommendation of the Association's Division of
Churches, initiated by George G. Davis that "it is desirable to
revive in some form the plan for organizing lay centers in communities where there is no Unitarian church and where there is a sufficient number of individual Unitarians, in general conformity with
the plan adopted in December, 1907. . . ." The idea fertilized in
committee during succeeding months. In October 1946 the Rev.
Lon Ray Call, the Association's minister-at-large, prepared and circulated a memorandum entitled "Unitarian Lay Groups" which cap-
tured the spirit and promise of the fellowships plan completely.[47]
Without realizing it Mr. Call had written the first comprehensive
statement of what a Unitarian fellowship could do and be. Within
a year the title "lay centers" was dropped in favor of "fellowship
groups" and on July 28, 1948 under the guidance of the Rev. Randall S. Hilton, Regional Director, and Munroe Husbands, now
Fellowship Director, the Unitarian Fellowship of Boulder, Colorado,
became the first "Unitarian fellowship" in the world.

In the consideration of Unitarian lay groups we must remember
that we have everything to gain and nothing to lose if the plan is well
conceived and carried out. We will lose everything we put into it
and will come out of it with lessened prestige unless it is well conceived and carried out. The project can be the most successful thing
the Unitarian Association has ever undertaken or it can be the most
dismal failure. There is no reason why there cannot be thousands of
Unitarian lay groups in the small cities, towns and villages of the
United States receiving regularly the ministrations of liberal religion
and working together in the advancement of the Unitarian movement. The Church of the Larger Fellowship doesn't touch directly
the lay group movement, but it could be of great assistance. Indeed,
each could help the other. . . .

A Unitarian lay group is not a forum. It is not a discussion club.
It is not a Sunday School. It is not a prayer meeting. It is not a
social club and it is not a church. It is disappointing to find when

the lay group idea is mentioned that so many confuse it with a plan
to provide a very poor substitute for a church service, with a sermon
at second hand to be read by someone present, and perhaps discussed
a little, with perhaps an introduction from a Scripture reading and
a concluding prayer. Among Unitarians such a plan would likely
lead only to failure.

It is necessary to think and plan to the end that a lay group may
be both a working unit and a spiritually satisfying organization. But
it is not a church and should not be thought of as being the first step
toward a church except in very promising cities.

As a working unit a lay group could do a considerable number of
constructive things. Its committee could be engaged in such varied
enterprises as (1) the distribution of Unitarian literature after the
fashion of the old Post Office Mission; (2) arranging for Unitarian
speakers at public meetings after the fashion of Christian Science
lecturers; (3) sponsoring local radio programs in places where there
are radio stations by transcription of carefully prepared addresses
designed for that specific purpose; (4) seeing that the town library
is supplied with the *Christian Register*, *Unity* and other Unitarian
periodicals and Unitarian books; (5) providing a local community
unit for the Unitarian Service Committee to collect food and cloth-
ing and aid in the money-raising campaigns; (6) cooperating with
the Commission on World Order and the Unitarian Fellowship of
Social Justice; (7) sending representatives to regional Unitarian conferences, summer institutes, etc.; (8) corresponding with kindred
spirits in other states. . . . These are but indications of what the lay
groups could do as working units.

Of course the primary function of a Unitarian lay group is to provide spiritually satisfying meetings for religious liberals in lieu of a
church in towns where in all probability religious liberalism is prac-
tically unknown. Unless we can do this and do it well we will fail.
I am convinced, however, that we can do it so well that in many
respects it will be as satisfying to the individual concerned as many a
church service. I am also convinced that it will provide our Unitarian movement with strength enough to more than offset the waning
virility of our churches.

Whatever we do must be as modern and interesting and challeng-
ing as is necessary to meet the competing interests of present day
people with their radios, movies and bridge games. What we provide should be unique, especially in its emphasis upon the creative

abilities of its members. People are suffering from a lack of spiritual creativity. They are subjected on every side to second-hand sermons as well as canned music and manufactured merriment. A Unitarian lay movement could be so planned as to encourage a great deal of creative religious activity. It could also go a long way toward getting over to its members the values preached in Unitarian pulpits Sunday after Sunday. . . .

This plan of establishing lay groups seems to me to be so important and so full of promise that it will justify a special department of the American Unitarian Association. . . .

Paralleling the new frontiers of Unitarian organization, there has emerged in addition a new frontier of faith. It has no name; it is not a party; it desires not controversy but the truth. In seeking an adequate religious faith in the present age, it seeks first of all to understand the realities of the present age. Therefore it is conceived not in optimism but in the chaos, suffering, and anxiety of the modern world. Believing that the traditional liberal answer of humanity's primary and ultimate dependence on its own powers to solve its problems has proved inadequate, it is willing to explore new sources of power and truth, most notably Christian theology, Existentialist philosophy, and the social and personality sciences.

A forerunner of this new movement of faith is James Luther Adams, professor of Christian Ethics at the Harvard Divinity School and for twenty years a teacher at the Meadville Theological School in the Federated Theological Faculty of the University of Chicago. Dr. Adams (with Christian presuppositions) affirms God to be the living, transforming reality in the lives of men and women and the reconstruction of society. His essay, "A Faith for Free Men," published in 1946, is recognized as an outstanding statement of contemporary liberal faith.[47]

The question concerning faith is not, "Shall I be a man of faith?" The proper question is, rather, "Which faith is mine?" or, better, "Which faith should be mine?" for, whether a person craves prestige, wealth, security, or amusement, whether he lives for country, for science, for God or for plunder, he shows that he has faith, he shows that he puts his confidence in something.

The faiths of the twentieth century have been as powerful and influential as any that have ever been. They have created its science and its atom bombs, its nationalisms and its internationalisms, its wars and its "peace," its heroisms and its despairs, its Hollywoods and its Broadways, its Wall Streets and its Main Streets, its Gestapos and its undergrounds, its democracies and its Fascisms, its socialisms and its communisms, its wealth and its poverty, its securities and its insecurities, its beliefs and its unbeliefs, its questions and its answers.

We must not believe every "pious" man's religion to be what he says it is. He may go to church regularly, he may profess some denominational affiliation, he may repeat his creed regularly, but he may actually give his deepest loyalty to something quite different from these things and from what they represent. Find out what that is and you have found his religion. You will have found his god. It will be the thing he gets most excited about, the thing that most deeply concerns him. But speak against it in the pulpit or in the Pullman car, and he may forget what he calls his religion or his god, and rush "religiously" to the defense of what really concerns him. The veins on his forehead will be distended, his eyes will flash, he will begin to raise his voice. What moves him now is more important than his creed or his atheism; it gives meaning and direction to his life. . . .

As creatures fated to be free, as creatures who must make responsible decision, what may we place our confidence in? What can we have faith in? What should we serve?

The first tenet of the free man's faith is that his ultimate dependence for his being and his freedom is upon a creative power and upon processes not of his own making. His ultimate faith is not in himself. He finds himself an historical being, a being living in nature and history, a being having freedom in nature and history. The forms that nature and history take possess a certain given, fateful character, and yet they are also fraught with meaningful possibilities.

Within this framework man finds something dependable and also many things that are not dependable. One thing that is dependable is the order of nature and of history which the sciences are able to describe with varying degrees of precision. . . .

Whatever the destiny of the planet or of the individual life, a sustaining meaning is discernible and commanding in the here and now. Anyone who denies this denies that there is anything worth taking seriously or even worth talking about. Every blade of grass, every work of art, every scientific endeavor, every striving for right-eousness bears witness to this meaning. Indeed, every frustration or perversion of truth, beauty or goodness also bears this witness, as the shadow points round to the sun.

One way of characterizing this meaning is to say that through it God is active or is fulfilling himself in nature and history. . . .

God (or that in which we may have faith) is the inescapable, commanding reality that sustains and transforms all meaningful existence. It is inescapable, for no man can live without somehow coming to terms with it. It is commanding, for it provides the structure or the process through which existence is maintained and by which any meaningful achievement is realized. . . . It is trans-forming, for it breaks through any given achievement, it invades any mind or heart open to it, luring it on to richer or more relevant achievement; it is a self-surpassing reality. God is that reality which works upon us and through us and in accord with which we can achieve truth, beauty or goodness. It is that reality which works in nature and history, under certain conditions creating human good in human community. Where these conditions are not met, human good, as sure as the night follows the day, will be frustrated or per-verted. . . .

This reality that is dependable and in which we may place our confidence is, then, not man—in it man lives and moves and has his being—nor is it a mere projection of human wishes; it is a work-ing reality that every man is coerced to live with. In this sense the faith of the free man is not free; man is not free to work without the sustaining, commanding reality. He is free only to obstruct it or to conform to the conditions it demands for growth. . . .

The free man's faith is therefore a faith in the giver of being and freedom. Man's dignity derives from the fact that he participates in the being and freedom of this reality. If we use the terms of historical Christianity we may say, man is made in the image of this creative reality. Under its auspices he becomes himself a creator. . . .

The second tenet of the free man's faith is that the commanding, sustaining, transforming reality finds its richest focus in meaningful human history, in free, co-operative effort for the common good. In other words, this reality fulfills man's life only when men stand in right relation to each other. Man, the historical being, comes most fully to terms with this reality in the exercise of the freedom that works for justice in the human community. Only what creates freedom in a community of justice is dependable. "Faith is the sister of justice." Only the society that gives every man the opportunity to share in the process whereby human potentiality is realizable, only the society that creates the social forms of freedom in a community of justice (where every man is given his due), only the freedom that respects the divine image and dignity in every man are dependable. As Lincoln put it, "Those who deny freedom to others deserve it not for themselves, and, under a just God, cannot long retain it."

A faith that is not the sister of justice is bound to bring men to grief. It thwarts creation, a divinely given possibility; it robs man of his birthright of freedom in an open universe; it robs the community of the spiritual riches latent in its members; it reduces man to a beast of burden in slavish subservience to a state, a church or a party—to a man-made God. That way lie the grinding rut and tyranny of the Vatican line, the Nuremberg line and the Moscow line, different though these lines are from each other in their fear and obstruction of freedom. . . .

Jesus uses the figure of the seed to describe this power. The power of God is like a seed that grows of itself if man will use his freedom to meet the conditions for its growth. It is not only a principle by which life may be guided; it is also a power that transforms life. It is a power we may trust to heal the wounds of life and to create the joy of sharing and of community. This is the power the Christian calls the forgiving, redemptive power of God, a power every man may know and experience whether or not he uses these words to describe it. . . .

The third tenet of the free man's faith is that the achievement of freedom in community requires the power of organization and the organization of power. The free man will be an unfree man, he will be a victim of tyranny from within or from without, if his free faith does not assume form, in both word and deed. The commanding, transforming reality is a shaping power; it shapes one's beliefs about that reality, and when it works through men it shapes the community of justice and love.

There is no such thing as poetry without poems, art without paintings, architecture without buildings, and there is no such thing as an enduring faith without beliefs. The living spirit, says the poet Schiller, creates and molds.

There can be no reliable faith for free men unless there are faithful men and women who form the faith into beliefs, who test and criticize the beliefs and who then transform and transmit the beliefs. This process of forming and transforming the beliefs of the free faith is a process of discussion; it is a co-operative endeavor in which men surrender to the commanding, transforming reality. The only way in which men can reliably form and transform beliefs is through the sharing of tradition and new insights and through the co-operative criticism and testing of tradition and insight. In other words, men must sincerely work with each other in order to give reliable form and expression to faith. This is the only way in which freedom from tyranny can be fulfilled in freedom with justice and truth. . . .

The free church is that community which is committed to determining what is rightly of ultimate concern to men of free faith. It is a community of the "faith-ful" and a community of sinners. When "alive," it is the community in which men are called to seek fulfillment by the surrender of their lives to the control of the commanding, sustaining, transforming reality. It is the community in which men are called to recognise and abandon their ever-recurrent reliance upon the unreliable. It is the community in which the living spirit of faith tries to create and mold life-giving, life-transforming beliefs, the community in which men open themselves to God and each other and to commanding, sustaining, transforming experiences from the past, appropriating, criticizing and transforming tradition and giving that tradition as well as newborn faith the occasion to become relevant to the needs of a time. . . .

Today we are living in a time of sifting. No mere "return to religion" in the conventional sense will give us the vision or the power to match the demands. "Return to religion" as usually understood restores only the ashes and not the fires of faith. In a time when we must determine whether we will have "One World or None," only a costing commitment to a tough faith in the commanding, sustaining, transforming power of God will even start us on the steep path towards a world in which there will be room for men of a free faith. If we can get such a world without a struggle for justice, it will, like an unexamined faith, not be worth having.

In fact, we shall not have it for long—for the Lord of history will not fail nor faint till he have set justice in the earth, until he have burst the cruel yoke asunder and given liberty to the captive and to them that are oppressed. This is the Lord of whom it is commanded, Thou shalt love the Lord thy God with all thy heart, and with all thy soul, and with all thy mind, and with all thy strength. Would any other Lord, of any name or no name, be lovable? If the men of a free faith do not love that commanding, sustaining, transforming reality, what else in heaven or earth could they or should they love? What else could they or should they have faith in?

Sources of the Documents

The Sixteenth Century

1. Michael Servetus, *The Two Treatises of Servetus on the Trinity*, trans. Earl Morse Wilbur (Cambridge, 1932 [quoted by permission of Harvard University Press]), pp. 6, 11-12, 17-18, 33-35, 45, 66-67, 103-104, 132, 100. See also Wilbur, *A History of Unitarianism: Socinianism and its Antecedents* (Cambridge, 1945), ch. 5, 9-13.

2. Quoted in Roland H. Bainton, *Hunted Heretic, the Life and Death of Michael Servetus* (Boston, 1953), pp. 207-209. See also Wilbur, *A History of Unitarianism*, ch. 9-12.

3. Eng. trans. by Roland H. Bainton (New York, 1935), pp. 125-126, 134-135, 149-150. See also Stefan Zweig, *The Right to Heresy: Castellio against Calvin* (Boston, 1951); and Wilbur, *A History of Unitarianism*, ch. 13-14.

4. Trans. by Selina Gerhard Schultz and published with her permission. See also her biography, *Caspar Schwenckfeld von Ossig* (1489-1561) (Norristown, Pa., 1946); and Joachim Wach, "Caspar Schwenckfeld," in *Types of Religious Experience* (Chicago, 1951), pp. 135-170.

5. Trans. from the Hungarian by Alexander St.-Ivanyi. See also Wilbur, *A History of Unitarianism in Transylvania, England, and America* (Cambridge, 1952), ch. 1-5.

6. Trans. by Alexander St.-Ivanyi from Elek Jakab, *The Life of Francis David* (Buda-Pest, 1879), p. 137. The original is in Latin and Hungarian.

The Seventeenth Century

7. *The Racovian Catechism; wherein You have the substance of the Confession of those Churches, which in the Kingdom of Poland, and Great Dukedom of Lithuania, and other Provinces appertaining to that Kingdom, do affirm, that no other save the Father of our Lord Jesus Christ, is that one God of Israel, and that the man Jesus of Nazareth, who was born of the Virgin, and no other besides, or before him, is the onely begotten Sonne of God* (Amsterdam, 1652), pp. 1, 8-9, 27-29, 70-71, 120-122. See also Wilbur, *A History of Unitarianism*, ch. 31.

8. (London, 1691), pp. 1, 4. See also H. John McLachlan, *Socinianism in Seventeenth-Century England* (London, 1951).

9. (London, 1691), pp. 1, 4, 8, 12, 17-18.

10. John Locke, *The Works of John Locke* (London, 1741), pp. 232, 234, 235, 242-243, 254-255. The volumes from which this and the following selection are taken were given to the Boston Public Library by Theodore Parker, and contain his marginal notations on Locke's writings.

11. John Locke, *The Works of John Locke* (London, 1714), II, pp. 530-531, 540-541.

The Eighteenth Century

12. Thomas Emlyn, *An Humble Inquiry into the Scripture Account of Jesus Christ: Or, a Short Argument concerning his Deity and Glory according to the Gospel*, in *A Collection of Tracts* by Thomas Emlyn, second ed. (London, 1731), pp. 3-6, 11-12, 45.

13. Thomas Belsham, *Memoirs of the late Rev. Theophilus Lindsey* (London, 1812), pp. 111-112. See also Wilbur, *A History of Unitarianism in Transylvania, England, and America*, ch. 12-15.

14. Theophilus Lindsey, *A second address to the students of Oxford and Cambridge relating to Jesus Christ and the origin of the great errors concerning him* (London, 1790), p. xix.

15. Joseph Priestley, *An History of the Corruptions of Christianity* (Birmingham, 1782), II, 440-443, I, 113-114. See also Wilbur, *A History of Unitarianism in Transylvania, England, and America*, ch. 16.

16. (Boston, 1743), pp. 35, 36, 50-51, 76-77, 79-80, 119-120, 126-127, 140, 142. See also Conrad Wright, *The Beginnings of Unitarianism in America* (Boston, 1955), especially ch. 1 and 2.

17. Jonathan Mayhew, *Seven Sermons upon the following subjects: viz. I. The Difference between the Truth and Falsehood, Right and Wrong. II. The natural Abilities of Men for discerning these Differences. III. The Right and Duty of Private Judgment. IV. Objections considered. V. The Love of God. VI. The Love of our Neighbor. VII. The first and great Commandment* (Boston, 1749), pp. 85-87. See also Wright, *The Beginnings . . .*, ch. 10 and throughout.

18. John Murray, *Letters and Sketches of Sermons* (Boston, 1812), II, 211, 212-213. See also Clarence Skinner and Alfred S. Cole, *Hell's Ramparts Fell, The Life of John Murray* (Boston, 1941); and Benjamin Hersey, "The Universalist Church in America," in *The Proceedings of the Unitarian Historical Society*, Vol. XI, Part II, pp. 5-26.

19. *Letters*, I, pp. 299-300.

20. *Letters*, I, p. 192.

21. *A Liturgy, collected principally from the Book of Common Prayer, for the use of the First Episcopal Church in Boston; together with the Psalter, or Psalms of David* (Boston, 1785). See also Henry Wilder Foote, *Annals of King's Chapel* (Boston, 1896), II, 380-393; also Wright, *The Beginnings . . .*, ch. 9.

22. *A Liturgy, collected principally from the Book of Common Prayer* (Boston, 1785), unnumbered pp. [3-4] and [20].

23. Adrienne Koch and William Peden (ed.), *The Life and Selected Writings of Thomas Jefferson* (New York: Modern Library, 1944), pp. 311-313.

24. Koch and Peden, *The Life and Selected Writings of Thomas Jefferson*, pp. 431-433.

The Nineteenth Century

25. Richard Wright, *A Review of the Missionary Life and Labors of Richard Wright* (London, 1824), pp. 72-79.

26. James Martineau, *Essays, Reviews and Addresses*, IV. Academical: Religious (London, 1891), pp. 570-571, 572-573, 574, 575-576, 577, 578, 579-580.

27. Jedidiah Morse, *The True Reasons on which the Election of a Hollis Professor of Divinity in Harvard College, was opposed at the Board of Overseers, Feb. 14, 1805* (Charlestown, 1805), pp. 19-21, 27-28. See also George E. Ellis, *A Half-Century of the Unitarian Controversy* (Boston, 1857).

28. Hosea Ballou, *A Treatise on Atonement* (Portsmouth, 1805), pp. 79-80, 235-236.

29. (Boston, 1815), second ed., pp. 11, 15-16, 17, 24, 37, 38-42.

30. *The Panoplist, and Missionary Magazine*, Vol. XI, No. 6, June, 1815, pp. 241-242, 250-251.

31. (Boston, 1948), pp. 18-19, 20, 23-27, 31-35, 40-41, 50-52, 58-59, 66-67, 76-77. See also Arthur W. Brown, *Always Young for Liberty, A Biography of William Ellery Channing* (Syracuse, 1956).

32. *Massachusetts Reports*, Vol. 16 (Boston, 1821), pp. 497-498, 500, 504, 513-514, 522.

33. (Boston, 1821), p. 1.

34. Henry Wilder Foote, *Thomas Jefferson, Champion of Religious Freedom, Advocate of Christian Morals* (Boston, 1947), pp. 62-63.

35. Koch and Peden, *The Life and Selected Writings of Thomas Jefferson*, pp. 703-704.

36. Manuscript in A.U.A. *Letter book, 1825* in the archives of the American Unitarian Association, Boston.

37. (Boston, 1955), pp. 1, 2-3, 5-6, 7-9, 10, 11-12, 17-18, 19, 21-22. See also Emerson's works, journals and letters in various editions; Ralph L. Rusk, *The Life of Ralph Waldo Emerson* (New York, 1949); and Perry Miller, *The Transcendentalists: An Anthology* (Cambridge, 1950).

38. (Boston, 1948), pp. 1, 6, 8-9, 28-30, 35-36, 39. See also Parker's *Works* (Boston, 1910), Centenary edition in fifteen volumes; and Henry S. Commager, *Theodore Parker, Yankee Crusader* (Boston, 1947).

39. Theodore Parker, *The Rights of Man in America* (Boston, 1911), pp. 147, 148-151, 152.

40. *Christian Register*, Vol. XLIV, No. 15, April 15, 1865, p. 58. See also George W. Cooke, *Unitarianism in America* (Boston, 1902), ch. 8.

41. *The Index* (Toledo, 1870), Vol. 1, No. 1, p. 1. See also Stow Persons, *Free Religion* (New Haven, 1947).

42. Jabez T. Sunderland, "The Issue in the West" (1886), pp. 2-4, 5, 6, 7, 13, 24-26, 42-43. See also Charles H. Lyttle, *Freedom Moves West* (Boston, 1952), Part III.

43. Quoted in Charles H. Lyttle, *Freedom Moves West* (Boston, 1952), pp. 189-190.

The Twentieth Century

44. Curtis W. Reese, *Humanism* (Chicago, 1926), pp. 55-63. See also Carleton Winston, *This Circle of Earth* (New York, 1942), a biography of Dietrich; and Charles Francis Potter, *The Preacher and I* (New York, 1951), especially ch. 28.

45. *The Humanist*, Vol. XIII, No. 2, March–April 1953, pp. 58-61. Reprinted by permission of "The American Humanist Association, Yellow Springs, Ohio." See also Charles E. Park, "Why the Humanism-Theism Controversy is Out of Date" (Boston, 1954), available as a pamphlet from the Division of Publications, 25 Beacon Street, Boston 8, Mass.

46. Commission of Appraisal, *Unitarians Face a New Age* (Boston, 1936), pp. 3-8.

47. Lon Roy Call, "Unitarian Lay Centers," mimeographed memorandum, Boston, October, 1946.

48. James Luther Adams, "A Faith for Free Men," in Stephen H. Fritchman (ed.), *Together We Advance* (Boston, 1946), pp. 50-51, 53, 54-55, 56-57, 58, 59-61, 64-65.

Index